What People Are Saying About Ap
Divine Encounter with the Holy Spirit...

Out of all the books I own on the topic of being filled with the Holy Spirit, I would rate Apostle Maldonado's new book, *Divine Encounter with the Holy Spirit*, at the very top of the list because it is the most practical and helpful for understanding the realities of ministry related to the Spirit. It is a great book, one that I will highly recommend to anyone wanting to grow in their understanding of the Holy Spirit, especially in regard to how to be led by the Spirit and how the Holy Spirit helps to create faith in our lives. I love a book that illustrates its truths with contemporary stories of people whom God is using. The truth creates in me knowledge and wisdom, and the stories create in me inspiration and hunger for more of God. Well done, Apostle Maldonado. Thank you for giving us wonderful insight into the things of God the Holy Spirit.

—*Randy Clark, D.Min., Th.D.*
Overseer, Apostolic Network of Global Awakening
Founder, Global Awakening

Divine Encounter with the Holy Spirit could also be called "Everything You Ever Wanted to Know about the Holy Spirit and Didn't Know to Ask." Apostle Maldonado explains the Person of the Holy Spirit and encourages you to realize that the Holy Spirit is your Best Friend—in fact, your best everything. This teaching opens the door for intimacy not only with the Holy Spirit but also with God the Father, His Son, His Word, and the supernatural. Renew or begin your relationship with the Holy Spirit through the revelations in this profound but simple book.

—*Marcus D. Lamb*
Founder and President, Daystar Television Network

We all want to see the transformative power that Jesus promises us, so that we would live a thriving and abundant life! We are believing for nations to be restored, cities to be transformed, and people to be empowered. There is a process we will have to engage, though—an intimate relationship with the Holy Spirit. I love that Apostle Guillermo Maldonado, who leads one of the largest Christian movements in the world, points at the divine encounters with the Holy Spirit as the access point to change the world. Our relationship with the Spirit of God is literally a game-changer, and if you can get the principles in this book activated in your life, you will see the fruit of this divine connection in your everyday world!

—*Shawn Bolz*
TV Personality and author, *Translating God*
www.bolzministries.com

Apostle Maldonado has been called by God to demystify the supernatural and make you naturally supernatural!

—*Sid Roth*
Host, *It's Supernatural!*

Apostle Guillermo Maldonado is one of the most outstanding people I've ever known. He is a Holy Spirit genius, and he is a living example of a man rooted in a deep relationship with the Spirit who daily lives with the result of his encounter. Such a divine encounter can also be yours.

—*Dr. Marilyn Hickey*
Marilyn Hickey Ministries

Divine Encounter with the Holy Spirit will release you into deep intimacy with God. Reading the book itself provokes supernatural experiences with God. Apostle Maldonado has lived the principles and insights he writes about in its pages and, as a result, has seen as many miracles as anyone in our modern-day era. I devoured *Divine Encounter*'s pages; it made me hungrier for the Holy Spirit, and it will do the same for you.

—*Dr. Cindy Jacobs*
Generals International

It is a blessing for me to endorse *A Divine Encounter with the Holy Spirit* and Apostle Guillermo Maldonado. This is the most crucial time in human history. Now more than ever before, we need to have a clear understanding of who the Holy Spirit is and how He works in us and through us to draw all men to Jesus Christ. I would urge you to get ahold of this book and not just read it but study it (2 Timothy 2:15). As you study, ask the Holy Spirit to give you a divine encounter with Him. May the eyes of your heart be flooded with revelatory light as you seek HIM (Ephesians 1:18)!

—*Bobby Conner*
Eagles View Global Ministries

One of the strongest encounters I have ever had with the Holy Spirit's visitation was in a meeting with Apostle Guillermo Maldonado. I have noticed a pattern with those who move in very powerful, supernatural demonstrations of God's glory, especially in healings and miracles, as Apostle Maldonado does. The common denominator is a strong intimacy with, and an understanding of, the Holy Spirit. Now, through his latest book, *Divine Encounter with the Holy Spirit*, you will learn from his personal moments with the Holy Spirit. You will also learn how to experience your own personal encounters that will help you touch this generation with the supernatural power of the Holy Spirit. Read the pages of this book and be prepared for a life of divine encounters with God's Spirit!

—*Hank Kunneman*
Lord of Hosts Church and One Voice Ministries

DIVINE ENCOUNTER

WITH THE

HOLY SPIRIT

GUILLERMO MALDONADO

WHITAKER
HOUSE

DIVINE ENCOUNTER WITH THE HOLY SPIRIT

Guillermo Maldonado
14100 SW 144th Ave.
Miami, FL 33186
kingjesus.org

ISBN: 978-1-62911-898-7
eBook ISBN: 978-1-62911-899-4
Printed in the United States of America
© 2017 by Guillermo Maldonado

Whitaker House
1030 Hunt Valley Circle
New Kensington, PA 15068
www.whitakerhouse.com

Library of Congress Cataloging-in-Publication Data (pending)

1 2 3 4 5 6 7 8 9 10 11 12 **UJ** 25 24 23 22 21 20 19 18 17

CONTENTS

INTRODUCTION:
GOD'S TRANSFORMATIVE
PRESENCE ON EARTH

Throughout the millennia of human history, God has progressively revealed Himself to humanity, manifesting His love, His divine characteristics, and His personhood, but especially His tripartite essence. He always reveals Himself as the one true God who exists in three Persons: God the Father, whom no man has seen (see John 1:18); God the Son, Jesus Christ, who is the Word made flesh that lived among us on earth (see John 1:14); and God the Holy Spirit, who continually guides, comforts, and empowers believers (see, for example, John 14:16). The Father dwells in the heavenly realm; Jesus is seated at the right hand of the Father, with the authority to govern the entire universe; and the Holy Spirit is active on earth, leading the church.

The Holy Spirit is the most overlooked member of the Trinity, yet His activity on earth is essential to us as believers. We ignore His work only to our great loss. We must have a renewed understanding of His divinity, His unity with the Father and the Son, and His indispensable work in our lives if we are to live in the fullness of God.

THE UNITY OF FATHER, SON, AND SPIRIT

The Holy Spirit coexists with the Father and the Son; He shares Their very essence and attributes, including omnipresence and omniscience. The Father is the Creator, or the Originator, of all that exists; the Son is the One who reveals the Father, and is also the Mediator for the human race; and the Holy Spirit is the Administrator of God's revelation and grace. The Three are equal, but They carry out different functions.

The Father bears witness of the Son (see John 5:37), the Son bears witness of the Father (see, for example, John 8:38; 14:7), and the Holy Spirit bears witness of the Son (see John 15:26). *"For there are three that bear witness in heaven: the Father, the Word, and the Holy Spirit; and these three are one"* (1 John 5:7). During His life on earth, Jesus spoke more of the Father than of Himself. Likewise, the Holy Spirit does not speak of Himself; He testifies of Jesus and of His finished work on the cross. The assignment of the Holy Spirit is to attest to Jesus on earth, just as the Son gives testimony of the Father who is in heaven.

Significantly, this means that when the Holy Spirit comes upon someone's life, Jesus is revealed to that person. It also means that if anyone teaches or preaches without exalting Jesus, what is spoken does not come from God, and the Holy Spirit does not support it. In order for the Holy Spirit to manifest the presence of God, Jesus must be revealed. When a preacher exalts Jesus, the Holy Spirit makes Himself present and confirms the divine origin of the message.

AN ACTIVE PARTICIPANT IN THE FATHER'S GREAT WORKS

In various passages, the Bible shows us that the Holy Spirit was an active participant in all of God's great works. We see that *"in the beginning God created the heavens and the earth.… And the Spirit of God moved upon the face of the waters"* (Genesis 1:1–2 KJV). Additionally, the Spirit was fully involved in the creation of humanity when God said, *"Let Us make man in Our image, according to Our likeness"* (Genesis 1:26; see also verse 27). He was specifically involved in the miraculous conception of Jesus, as the angel explained to Mary: *"The Holy Spirit will come upon you, and the power of the Highest will overshadow you; therefore, also, that Holy One who is to be born will be called the Son of God"* (Luke 1:35). We also see the Holy Spirit participating in the work of salvation that Jesus completed on the cross. In Hebrews 9:13–14, we read,

> *For if the blood of bulls and goats and the ashes of a heifer, sprinkling the unclean, sanctifies for the purifying of the flesh, how much more shall the blood of Christ, who through the eternal Spirit offered Himself without spot to God, cleanse your conscience from dead works to serve the living God?*

Likewise, He was present at the resurrection of Christ; that is why Scripture says, *"But if the Spirit of Him who raised Jesus from the dead dwells in you, He who raised Christ from the dead will also give life to your mortal bodies through His Spirit who dwells in you"* (Romans 8:11). We also see the Spirit taking a direct part in the birth of the church:

> *When the Day of Pentecost had fully come, [Jesus' followers] were all with one accord in one place. And suddenly there came a sound from heaven, as of a rushing mighty wind, and it filled the whole house where they were sitting. Then there appeared to them divided tongues, as of fire, and one sat upon each of them. And they were all filled with the Holy Spirit and began to speak with other tongues, as the Spirit gave them utterance.* (Acts 2:1–4)

As God's transformative presence on earth, the Holy Spirit continues to be an active participant in His great works, especially the regeneration of believers in their spirits, souls, and bodies to become the pure bride of Christ, and their empowerment to spread the gospel of the kingdom. In the same way that Jesus ministered on earth, the Holy Spirit ministers on earth today, doing the will of the Father who sent Him. This keeps the three persons of the Trinity in complete and constant unity, because They work for the same purpose and from the same mind. Again, the Three are indivisible, and the only differences between them are the functions They fulfill and their realms of operation.

Through *Divine Encounter with the Holy Spirit*, you will come to understand many essential truths about God's Spirit and your relationship to Him. You will learn the answers to questions many believers are asking, such as: What are the characteristics of the Holy Spirit? What are the Spirit's functions, and what is their purpose? How does the Holy Spirit flow among us? How do we know that we are truly under the Spirit's leadership and guidance? How does the Holy Spirit draw us closer to the Father and Jesus? Additionally, you will discover how the survival of the church today depends on our understanding of the fundamental role of the Holy Spirit in the events of the end times—which have brought about His present outpouring—and how He moves over the face of the earth and in our lives.

I now invite you to a *divine encounter with the Holy Spirit* through which you can establish a personal, intimate, and transformative relationship with God in all His fullness—as Father, Son, and Holy Spirit.

1

A SUPERNATURAL ENCOUNTER
WITH THE HOLY SPIRIT

According to the recorded history of the Bible, every person who was called by God had a supernatural encounter with Him. In each case, the encounter was personal and unique.

God called Abraham with an audible voice. (See, for example, Genesis 12:1–3; 17:1–22.) He appointed Jacob through a dream (see Genesis 28:10–17), and Joseph through two dreams (see Genesis 37:5–10). He commissioned Moses through a burning bush (see Exodus 4:4–6), and Isaiah through a vision of God's throne (see Isaiah 6:1–5). He called Paul through the audible voice of Jesus, accompanied by the brilliance of His divine glory. (See Acts 9:3–19.)

Additionally, all the men and women who were called and used by God had this in common: they impacted their generations, territories, societies, governments, and nations with the kingdom of God. What triggered the impact for each was their supernatural encounter with the Lord through His Holy Spirit.

In our day, God continues to use supernatural methods to commission and empower His people to impact the world for His kingdom. As He did for those we read about in the Bible, He gives each of us our own experience and calls us in a personal and distinct way. He may use angelic visions, dreams, and even dramatic experiences with heaven or hell, to prepare us to endure adversity, persecution, rejection, and betrayal in relation to our calling. In the midst of all these trials, the supernatural encounter gives us the strength to persevere while filling us with holy awe.

In my case, He spoke out loud to me and gave me this specific assignment: "I have called you to bring My supernatural power to this generation." Since then, I have turned all my efforts in that direction. The power and presence of God do not work randomly, but always with a clear purpose. He wants to demonstrate His supernatural power through us, and in order for that to happen, He gives us an encounter with the Holy Spirit according to the unique purposes He has for us.

Everyone must humbly accept the way in which God calls them, in order to complete His commission for them on the earth.

CHANGE, EMPOWERMENT, AND IMPACT

Every supernatural encounter with God includes change, empowerment, and impact. It involves a manifestation, whether visible or invisible, in which God introduces Himself to us in such a way that our heart is radically transformed, and we are empowered to impact our generation. The revelation that God gives is not for the purpose of making us more intelligent or admired, but to enable us to encounter Him daily, as Adam and Eve did in the garden of Eden (see Genesis 3:8), and receive fresh anointings. He wants us to have continual, intimate encounters with Him—not something sporadic or infrequent—in which we are face-to-face with the presence of God through His Spirit.

> ## Man was created to live in the presence of God and to carry it wherever he goes.

In the pages of the New Testament, we meet Saul of Tarsus (later called Paul)—a very educated man who is believed to have had one of the most developed minds of his time, who could quote the Torah from beginning to end, and who knew the tradition of Israel well and was zealous for the Law. Yet we find that none of his accomplishments changed his heart or transformed his life, because he had not yet received the revelation of who Jesus was. This demonstrates how a person can have the truth about God in their mind but not in their heart. If you have not experienced significant personal transformation, it is because the Word of God has not been fully revealed to you—or you have not accepted it. You may be someone who studies much about God but does not really *know* Him; you read about His kingdom, but you do not live in it.

Paul's calling shows us the path to change, empowerment, and impact. He was a religious zealot and a legalist before meeting Jesus. He even believed that imprisoning Christians honored God! (See Acts 8:3.) However, when he had an encounter with Jesus through the power of the Holy Spirit, his repentance and transformation were such that he became the greatest apostle in history, impacting much of the known world in his time and writing thirteen books of the New Testament.

This is how Paul found himself face-to-face with Jesus the Messiah:

Then Saul, still breathing threats and murder against the disciples of the Lord, went to the high priest and asked letters from him to the synagogues of Damascus, so that if he found any who were of the Way, whether men or women, he might bring them bound to Jerusalem. As he journeyed he came near Damascus, and suddenly a light shone around him from heaven. Then he fell to the ground, and heard a voice saying to him, "Saul, Saul, why are you persecuting Me?" And he said, "Who are You, Lord?" Then the Lord said, "I am Jesus, whom you are persecuting. It is hard for you to kick against the goads." So he, trembling and astonished, said, "Lord, what do You want me to do?" Then the Lord said to him, "Arise and go into the city, and you will be told what you must do." (Acts 9:1–6)

From the moment Paul had that encounter with Jesus, he changed completely. His transformation was multidimensional, affecting all areas of his life: his way of thinking, feeling, and living. It was a radical change!

For some, having an encounter with God results in immediate, drastic change; for others, the change is progressive. Likewise, some people may instantly understand the revelation they have received in an encounter with God; they appropriate it and carry out His call or instruction, as Paul later did when he was warned by God in a vision to leave Jerusalem. (See Acts 22:17–18.) Others may take time to realize the presence of God and His revelation, similar to what Jacob expressed in Genesis 28:16: *"Surely the Lord is in this place, and I did not know it."*

TYPES OF ENCOUNTERS WITH THE HOLY SPIRIT

Before the coming of Jesus, encounters with God were reserved mainly for those who had a key role in upbuilding God's people Israel and participating in His unfolding plan of salvation for humanity, paving the way for the Messiah. However, after Christ was resurrected and seated at the right hand of the Father, He sent the Holy Spirit to remain with *all* believers and to continue His ministry on earth. We can now have supernatural encounters with the Spirit of God, not as an isolated event, but as a lifestyle.

Based on the way they originate, we can identify two general types of supernatural encounters:

1. Those given by God in His sovereignty.

2. Those sought by God's children who are hungry and thirsty for Him.

ENCOUNTERS GIVEN BY GOD IN HIS SOVEREIGNTY

Many Christians in the Western world may feel that having an encounter with the living God is either optional or "available upon request." Their attitudes are seriously flawed, but at least they know that an encounter is possible. And God may still choose to reveal Himself sovereignly to His people even if they aren't seeking Him. But what about those who don't know God, living in nations where Christianity is not well-known, widely practiced, or legal? How can people in these countries seek encounters with God through the Holy Spirit if they have never even heard of Him and don't know how to reach out to Him? This is a special type of situation where the Lord will sovereignly grant people divine encounters.

The following are several testimonies that were related to me by people who attended a Supernatural Encounter conference that I held in India. None of them had experienced God until the Lord miraculously revealed Himself to them in a divine encounter.

Ryan is a young Hindu man who had never seen or read a Bible until he had a vision one night. He explained that during this vision, "I sat at the feet of Jesus, and He read Psalm 91, saying, 'This is My word to you.' The next day, my father and I read that chapter of the Bible together.

My father was very happy that his son had heard the voice of God and learned a part of the Scriptures, but I said to him, 'Papa, I have never read or opened the Bible before; Jesus appeared to me in a vision.' How can I relate what happened to me? I can only describe it as His glory. I did not know who the Holy Spirit was. I could not see the face of the Person who spoke to me; all I saw was light. His clothes were bright light and His feet, too, but I knew it was Jesus."

A Hindu woman from Dubai testified that when she was twenty-eight years old, she'd had a similar experience even though she was not Christian: "As I slept, a bright light entered my room, and when I awoke I saw Jesus standing in front of me. My room was filled with white light, and He was wearing a white robe and had His arms wide open. I could see that His hands had nail holes, and when I looked at His feet, I saw blood. All He said was, 'Come to Me, I am waiting for you.' At that time, I was Hindu; but just a while ago, while we were praying and I had my hands up, I felt as if someone was holding my hands, and I again saw that bright, white light. I saw Jesus before me while we were praying!"

Another striking testimony is that of Matthew, a Hindu businessman, who had faced serious financial problems and come close to committing suicide by driving his car off a cliff, not having acknowledged Jesus as his Lord and Savior. Sometimes, something supernatural happens only when a person reaches a point where they can no longer continue the way they have been. Then the Holy Spirit leads them to know the Father and His Son Jesus Christ. This was what Matthew testified:

"When I was thirty years old, I was driving one day, overwhelmed by large debts I could not pay, when my car was filled with something I could not explain. I believe it was the glory of God. I could see Jesus sitting beside me, looking at me. I do not have words to describe it. It was so real that I felt I could touch Him, and I heard Him clearly say, 'Do you not believe in Me? I am the One who freed the people of Israel, and for forty years I sustained them without their lacking anything. My son, you are only one person; how can I not take care of you too?'

"I felt like I would have a heart attack from all the raw emotions I felt, so I stopped my car by the side of the road, and I went out and sat on the ground. I did not know what was happening. Then I got back in my car and made a U-turn, leaving behind the cliff I had been about to throw myself from, and I said to Him, 'Jesus, I want to remember this place always.' I was still in the midst of a financial struggle, but now I knew that God was in control of my life. A week later, a man I did not know knocked on my door and handed me paperwork; it was the title to my house! He simply said it was a gift to me, and then he left. From that moment, my life turned around. Now I am an apostle of Jesus Christ. I pastor a church of more than seventy-five thousand people, and God continues to manifest in my life."

ENCOUNTERS SOUGHT BY GOD'S CHILDREN WHO ARE HUNGRY AND THIRSTY FOR HIM

The second type of supernatural encounter is one directly sought by God's people. While many divine encounters reported in the Bible were unexpected, like Paul's on the road to Damascus, others were diligently pursued, as in the case of the woman suffering from the flow of blood. (See, for example, Luke 8:43–48.) In fact, Jesus Himself sought an encounter with God the Father when He went to the Jordan to be baptized by John. (See, for example, Matthew 3:13–17.)

I want to reaffirm that there is no limit to the number of times one can have a supernatural encounter with the Holy Spirit, nor to who can have them. However, as we will further see, our experience with Him will depend on the degree of spiritual hunger and thirst we have. Encounters are a promise to all believers, and are available twenty-four hours a day. If they are not sovereignly given by God, we can seek them, because they are promised in the Scriptures.

Some years ago, while in a hotel in Colombia, I was preparing for a great crusade when I had an encounter with God as Father. As I prayed, I suddenly heard footsteps, as if someone had entered my room. Then I heard the voice of God say to me, "You know Me as Savior, but you do not know Me as your Father." At that moment, I began to cry uncontrollably. I had been in the ministry for several years, but I still held on to many fears and feelings of rejection; I constantly dealt with insecurities, both ministerial and personal. But that supernatural encounter with God as my Father changed my life completely. He told me, "From your loins will come children who will impact the world with My supernatural power." And so it has been and continues to be fulfilled in my life.

By His grace, I have raised up thousands of spiritual sons and daughters throughout the world. Today, they are successful people who impact the world in more than forty countries, bringing transformation to the nations, governments, and societies where they live. They lead powerful churches and ministries of all sizes, with miracles, signs, and wonders. All of this is due to my receiving the fatherhood of God in that encounter. Tens of thousands of lives have been transformed because I received the Spirit of adoption by which I call God *"Abba, Father"* (Romans 8:15). He erased all my insecurities and led me to believe in men and women who needed to accept the same fatherhood to fulfill the Lord's purpose in their own lives. All of this has led me to live with a constant desire to know God more and to receive more from Him to minister to others—and supernatural encounters with His Holy Spirit are the key to receiving what I need.

THE PROGRESSION OF A SUPERNATURAL ENCOUNTER

While there are many aspects to a supernatural encounter with God, we can summarize the process as having three fundamental stages:

1. AN IMPACT BRINGING PERMANENT CHANGE AND EMPOWERMENT

When someone has a genuine personal encounter with Jesus Christ as their Savior, their heart is impacted by God's love and grace, and the certainty of knowing they need to be forgiven and rescued by Him. But after salvation, they need impactful encounters with the Holy Spirit that bring empowerment for transformation and service. If their encounter with Jesus as Savior is not followed by regular encounters with the Holy Spirit, they run the risk of losing the fruit of the salvation encounter—and that fruit is permanent change.

Yet how many Christians are under the impression that having a single encounter with Christ as their Savior is enough? Some believers simply think there is nothing more to look for, but there are others who harden their hearts and are satisfied with only the initial encounter of salvation. The truth is that God wants to reveal Himself to us in a continuous way as the Almighty One—as our Father, Provider, Miracle Worker, Healer, Protector, Defender, Deliverer, and Supplier of everything we need!

2. A PROFOUND DESIRE FOR MORE OF GOD'S PRESENCE

An encounter with the Holy Spirit also provides the very thing that most believers are missing in their lives—a deep desire for the continual presence of God. That is why those who have a divine encounter suddenly feel an insatiable longing for more of God, and they begin to seek and pursue Him. They do not want to live outside of His presence—nor return to the world, to loneliness, or to sin and evil. This permanent desire for more of God opens the doors for the Holy Spirit to further work within them and through them.

> **A desire for more of God guarantees divine supernatural activity. Wherever there is a lack of hunger for God, the Lord has nothing to work with.**

3. A LEVEL OF IMPACT DETERMINED BY THE LEVEL OF HEART TRANSFORMATION

When someone enters a new level of relationship with the Lord through a divine encounter, the power of the Spirit begins to operate in them. I mentioned earlier that this produces either instantaneous or gradual changes—and this depends on the degree to which people allow the encounter to influence them. In other words, the encounter with the Holy Spirit leads them to experience a transformation that is as drastic or dramatic as the encounter itself and the hunger for God it has impelled in them.

It is true that any encounter with God may produce a greater or lesser impact in someone's life because we are all different, and He treats us all in a special way. However, the point I want to emphasize here is that we can hinder the power or immediacy of the impact by resisting God's work or by holding on to self-centered ambition or selfish motivations. The Bible shows us that out of the twelve disciples of Jesus, all continued to follow His steps—except one. Judas was disappointed because his encounter with Jesus did not turn out the way he had expected; he may have anticipated Jesus ruling over a political kingdom rather than a spiritual one. Besides that, he was controlled by greed. In the end, he sold Jesus to be killed because he did not accept the reality that an encounter with the Son of God must always be radically life-changing. That is why Jesus said to His disciples, *"Did I not choose you, the twelve, and one of you is a devil?"* (John 6:70).

The level of change will always be proportional to the impact of the supernatural encounter.

People might experience a low level of impact in their lives following a divine encounter because they have only been "touched" but not truly changed. We must always keep alert to this possibility and guard against it. Let us return to the case of Judas as an example. He had an initial encounter with Jesus and then walked with Him for three and a half years as His disciple. He saw Jesus perform miracles and signs, including the resurrection of the dead and the supernatural multiplication of food to feed the multitudes. He heard all of Jesus' teachings and was a recipient of the love of the Father, which Jesus imparted to all equally. Judas could even say that he had been used by Christ to give sight to the blind and hearing to the deaf, and to cast out demons. Jesus had treated him just as He had all His other disciples. But although Judas had been exposed to the presence and power of God, he never permitted these encounters to produce real transformation in his heart. *Judas was touched, but not changed.*

Centuries earlier, when the people of Israel were delivered from Egypt, Pharaoh was touched by the Lord's demonstrations of power. As a result, when he saw the plague of locusts consuming the land's harvests, *"Pharaoh called for Moses and Aaron in haste, and said, 'I have sinned against the LORD your God and against you. Now therefore, please forgive my sin only this once, and entreat the LORD your God, that He may take away from me this death only'"* (Exodus 10:16–17). Pharaoh was touched but not transformed, because as soon as he was free from the plague, his heart became hardened again, refusing to do God's will. He saw every one of the plagues strike the land, and he even saw his firstborn die, yet he still went out to persecute the people he had just liberated. That is why he ended up losing his entire army at the bottom of the Red Sea.

The people of Israel who were delivered from Pharaoh had a similar heart issue. They were touched by God with the signs and wonders He did. However, during their forty years in the desert, they constantly complained, rebelled, and turned away from the Lord. This proves that real change never took place within them. That is why the law of Moses was written on stone tablets—as a way to symbolize the hardness of the Israelites' hearts.

By contrast, when the prophet Isaiah saw the glory of God, he was so impacted that he was immediately overcome with conviction:

> *So I said: "Woe is me, for I am undone! Because I am a man of unclean lips, and I dwell in the midst of a people of unclean lips; for my eyes have seen the King, the LORD of hosts." Then one of the seraphim flew to me, having in his hand a live coal which he had taken with the tongs from the altar. And he touched my mouth with it, and said: "Behold, this has touched your lips; your iniquity is taken away, and your sin purged."* (Isaiah 6:5–7)

Isaiah felt the full impact of that divine encounter and opened his heart to it. He immediately recognized his condition as a sinner; and, nearly seven hundred years before Jesus' coming, his sins were forgiven. His transformation was such that he became the voice of God for his time and for generations to come.

Is it possible that someone in our day might allow themselves to be only touched by God but not changed? Although it seems incredible, we see many people like Judas and Pharaoh in today's church. Despite being touched by the Holy Spirit, they harden their hearts and don't allow Him to transform them within. When someone has a true encounter with the Holy Spirit, it sparks within them a burning desire and a strong passion to seek and receive more of God. It continually impacts their life. Today, God wants you to have genuine encounters with His Spirit that will transform your life!

The aspects of our lives where we resist change are those in which God is not wanted; the Spirit cannot flow there or give life to us in those areas.

GOD'S PURPOSES FOR SUPERNATURAL ENCOUNTERS

Now that we know how much God wants to give us supernatural encounters with His Holy Spirit, let's take a deeper look at His specific purposes for these encounters. Everything that God does has a purpose. Nothing in Him is random, including supernatural encounters and the impartation of His power. Encounters with the Spirit of God are given for the following reasons.

1. TO CAUSE US TO LOSE AWARENESS OF OURSELVES SO GOD CAN BECOME OUR COMPLETE REALITY

We have seen that the level of impact that an encounter has on an individual depends on the degree to which that person is willing to yield before the Holy Spirit. That means it is determined by how much they surrender to God's will, how much they give up their self-serving desires and thoughts, how much they are controlled by the Spirit rather than by the fleshly nature, and how much they rely fully on the Lord. To do these things, they must release their self-consciousness, or awareness of themselves (both of their strengths and their weaknesses).

> **The proof of a supernatural encounter with the Holy Spirit is that we have taken the focus off ourselves and gained a greater desire for the presence of God.**

Adam wasn't aware of his nakedness until he took his eyes off God. When he and his wife, Eve, sinned, *"the eyes of both of them were opened, and they realized they were naked"* (Genesis 3:7 NIV). In a related way, many people are so self-conscious and self-centered that they have completely lost their awareness of God. Human nature always wants to be in control of everything, but we must trust the Spirit of God and submit wholly to Him. We can do this when we take the focus off ourselves. Giving control to the Spirit is the only way to become fully aware of God and His Holy Spirit.

2. TO CHANGE AND TRANSFORM OUR HEART

And we all, who with unveiled faces contemplate the Lord's glory, are being transformed into his image with ever-increasing glory, which comes from the Lord, who is the Spirit. (2 Corinthians 3:18 NIV)

As we saw from the examples of Isaiah and the apostle Paul, when someone has a genuine supernatural encounter, it causes such an impact that it transforms the person's heart and life. People who have been changed in this way are empowered to impact the society in which they live. Additionally, it is impossible for someone who has had an encounter with the Spirit of God to be content with going back to their old way of living—to a lifestyle of sin; to being separated from the Father; to abusing drugs or alcohol; to being involved in sexual immorality; to living in depression, poverty, or illness; to being bound by curses, hatred, or envy; or to participating in any other destructive practices they had left behind.

It is true there are people who, following an encounter with God, return to mere religion, tradition, or dead churches where the Holy Spirit is rejected. Even after experiencing the supernatural, they return to the natural. This means they were touched, but not changed, by the encounter, as expressed earlier.

When you have a divine encounter with the Holy Spirit, you experience a spiritual reality that you had not known before. Once you know that reality, you are responsible for living in it, because it is the atmosphere of true life. If you go back to the world, you run serious risks; your physical life is even in danger. If you return to tradition, religion, or the old environment from which you were set free, it can cost you your family and even your salvation. I know many people who have gone back who are now divorced, sick, poor, depressed, discouraged, and empty of the life of God. When we turn away from the Holy Spirit's work in our lives, we will stop progressing, stagnate, and live outside of our true identity and purpose. For me, that is not life!

If you continue to struggle with sin or oppression without being able to overcome it, you urgently need to have an encounter with the Holy Spirit. Cry out to God for a *transformational* encounter. In a divine encounter, we receive a freedom that we cannot find outside of Him. His presence brings us revelation of the throne of God and of the abundant life that only He can give us. In fact, it is impossible to live in God's presence without changing spiritually, mentally, emotionally, and physically.

A person who is transformed by the Holy Spirit is imparted with eternal life, in the presence of God.

The important thing is that we remain in a state of continuous change, through frequent supernatural encounters. Being continuously transformed by the Spirit is tied to our integrity to live according to the spiritual realities that we believe in, experience, and proclaim. This point is especially crucial for ministers. Ministers are called to guide believers, and they should preach God's Word continually; however, they should also *experience* these messages *before* they preach them. They cannot talk about the Holy Spirit without first knowing Him themselves, or they will fail to lead anyone else to know Him.

Why is this? Because it is God's will for us to impart His life, His holiness, and His kingdom to others in order to change lives. In the kingdom of God, spiritual truth is not merely taught to people; it is *imparted* to them as they receive the revelation and experience the spiritual reality. God knows that if we preach without having experienced the supernatural power that moves us to change, the forces of darkness will accuse us of preaching about an area in which we have not been transformed. And God, as the righteous Judge, will not be able to keep us from the consequences, because we will be operating outside of His grace.

All preachers must therefore have a genuine transformation before they go into the pulpit to teach others about how to live according to the Word of God. If I have not been impacted or transformed before I preach a truth, I have no authority to teach it, because it is not a reality for me. That word will not contain the life of the Holy Spirit that can be revealed in people because, again, the Spirit works only within a realm of integrity. Operating outside the life of the Spirit leads us to live according to religion rather than according to God's transforming truth. Thus, when God gives us a revelation, we must allow His Spirit to work a change in our heart in relation to it. Then He will manifest Himself to our listeners, transforming and empowering them, as we proclaim that revelation.

 After an encounter with the Holy Spirit, the supernatural becomes a lifestyle.

3. TO CAUSE JESUS TO BECOME REAL IN US

Additionally, an encounter with the Holy Spirit makes Jesus real in our lives. In fact, this is mandatory and essential for every believer—and especially every minister of God. Christ must be more real to us than the people we minister to. If God the Father, Jesus, and the Holy Spirit had not been more real to me than the people I have preached to, I would have thrown in the towel a while ago! Many have betrayed me, spoken ill of me, and rejected me, but because God is more real to me than they are, I have been enabled to continue to obey my calling.

In the times in which we live, with the circumstances and challenges we face every day, we have to be sure that the risen Christ is more real to us than everyone and everything else. He is more real than illness, oppression, depression, financial lack, marital problems, and the ungratefulness and betrayals of others. Christ is eternally real!

Which is more real to you? Your problem, your sin, your fear, your sickness—or the Son of God? Is Jesus more real to you than people's criticism and persecution?

Without the Holy Spirit, we will surrender to difficult circumstances.

When Moses had an encounter with the fire of God (see Exodus 3), the Lord became more real to him than Egypt's Pharaoh or his advisors, more real to him than Egypt's sorcerers, and more real to him than the length and depth of the waters of the Red Sea (see Exodus 14). Moses needed that supernatural encounter so he would know that God was greater than all the circumstances and persecutions he would face. The supernatural nature of the demonic is based on lies and deception—it is false and counterfeit. But the supernatural realm of God is based on the truth—it is both *true* and *real*.

At present, the transforming power of the Holy Spirit is no longer recognized in many churches because the truth about Him is not being preached, but the Holy Spirit wants to become real in our lives and to make Jesus real to us. Jesus is *"the way, the truth, and the life"* (John 14:6). As a believer, you have the nature of God within you, but let me ask you again: How real is that nature to you? How real is Jesus and His finished work on the cross to you?

The Holy Spirit is *"the Spirit of truth"* (John 14:17). When we have an encounter with the Holy Spirit, He brings the reality of Eden back into our lives. In this reality, we know who created us and where we belong, and we understand the power that is at our disposal. The Spirit reveals to us that the Word of God is true; that Jesus Christ and His atoning blood are real; that the Father, His anointing, and His presence are real. We also understand that the devil, sin, and the flesh are real—but can and must be conquered in Christ.

Any area of our lives not under the influence of the Holy Spirit will be under the control of our flesh, the system of this world, and the devil. In this situation, the flesh, the world, and the devil become more real to us than the Holy Spirit. When our inner reality is ungodliness, fear, or a religious mind-set, that is what will be reflected externally. We will lack peace and power. In Paul's letter to Timothy, we read about people *"having a form of godliness but denying its power"* (2 Timothy 3:5). After we have a true encounter with the Holy Spirit, we will not merely have a "form" of godliness. Jesus will become real in us, the reality of heaven will come back to life for us, and God's kingdom will be manifested outwardly through us.

The spiritual reality within us will manifest as our natural, external reality.

4. TO EMPOWER AND COMMISSION US TO DEMONSTRATE THE SUPERNATURAL

At His baptism, Jesus received both the Father's commission and His empowerment to fulfill His ministry on earth. Likewise, when we have a divine encounter with the Holy Spirit, we are commissioned to go and demonstrate the supernatural power of God in the realm of our purpose and calling. God speaks to us personally and gives us a specific assignment; this assignment is confirmed through someone who is in spiritual authority over us, and who is under spiritual authority themselves—such as an apostle, prophet, pastor, or other leader. This is what gives us the legal right to use the power we have received in that encounter.

In a supernatural encounter, we are empowered and activated; and when we are commissioned, we are also delegated authority.

Our spiritual authority comes from Jesus. When the Son of God rose from the dead, He defeated death and Satan, and He received all authority from the Father: *"And Jesus came and spoke to* [His disciples], *saying, 'All authority has been given to Me in heaven and on earth'"* (Matthew 28:18). It is Jesus' authority that has been delegated to us. We are authorized to demonstrate the power of God and the finished work of Christ on the cross. After experiencing divine encounters with the Holy Spirit, we can overcome Satan; heal the sick; deliver the oppressed; perform miracles, signs, and wonders; and participate in many other ways to carry out God's purposes in the world. We have authority to do great works—*the works that Christ did, and even more* (see John 14:12)—so that the "impossible" begins to be possible (see, for example, Mark 9:23). In this hour, I declare upon you a supernatural encounter with the Holy Spirit, and in the name of Jesus, I activate and empower you to do miracles, signs, and wonders.

Ever since the victory of Jesus on the cross, being empowered, activated, and commissioned is a gift for every believer.

5. TO ENABLE US TO BECOME CARRIERS OF THE SUPERNATURAL

A further purpose of divine encounters is to allow us to become carriers of the supernatural. A supernatural carrier is a person who bears the spiritual legacy of a generation in order to transfer it to others. It is someone who brings with them the power and presence of God, transforming atmospheres and quickening environments with God's glory wherever they go, and manifesting miracles, signs, and wonders. When Moses had his encounter with the fire of God, he became the bearer of that fire; as a result, he was filled with the divinely-given passion to free God's people, and he worked miracles in Egypt and in the wilderness, where the glory of God, as a pillar of fire, led the Israelites continuously. (See Exodus 7–15.)

Likewise, when you have a divine encounter, you are authorized to demonstrate the power of God wherever you set foot. Are you ready to do it? If you are, your main commission is the one that Jesus gave His followers: *"Go into all the world and preach the gospel to every creature"* (Mark 16:15).

The apostle Peter was a fisherman with no formal education, but after his encounter with the Holy Spirit at the Feast of Pentecost, his transformation was so great that he became a carrier of the supernatural power of God. In fact, he carried the power of God to such an extent that people *"brought the sick out into the streets and laid them on beds and couches, that at least the shadow of Peter passing by might fall on some of them"*

(Acts 5:15). In and of itself, a shadow has no power; this is why we know it was the Holy Spirit, flowing from inside of Peter, who healed the sick. Similarly, Paul went from being a cruel persecutor of Christians to being a compassionate servant of Christ, and Scripture says that even cloths and aprons he had used were a means by which the sick were healed and evil spirits were cast out of people. (See Acts 19:11–12.) I am sure that if God could raise up an uneducated fisherman like Peter and a religious fanatic like Paul to confirm His Word through signs and wonders, He can also lift you up to become a carrier of His supernatural power.

The types of miraculous works recorded in the Bible continue to happen in our day among those who are carriers of the supernatural, because the power of God is the same yesterday, today, and forever. (See Hebrews 13:8.) This reality is clearly evidenced by the testimony of Pastor Maximiliano Leiva from the Centro Cristiano Internacional (International Christian Center) in the city of Formosa, Argentina. Pastor Leiva told me of a powerful creative miracle that occurred after he attended one of our leadership conferences at King Jesus International Ministry in Miami. This is his testimony:

"One day, you preached about how the supernatural power of God can work miracles of healing and deliverance in the now, and at the end of the service you passed out cloths anointed with oil to be given to the sick so they could receive the healing power of God. I brought several of these cloths back to Argentina and distributed them to the leaders of my church, one of whom knew a man who had been suffering from leprosy for fifteen years. The man's flesh had deteriorated to such a degree that he looked like a living corpse. His whole body had a gray appearance; his skin was dry, with scales, sores, and scabs, and his flesh was slipping off of him. Everyone knew the man was about to die. But this church leader gave him the cloth and told him of the great power, love, and mercy of God for His children.

"The leprous man, repentant and broken, took the cloth and, with great faith, prayed to God for his healing. The next day, he was greatly surprised to find his body healthy—completely clear of leprosy. In less than twenty-four hours, God had healed him and given him new skin! Now made whole, and full of joy and gratitude, he went to the church to testify and give thanks to God. All were amazed at such a miracle."

Can a piece of cloth anointed with oil heal someone? No! But the supernatural power of God contained within it can do that—and much more. Truly, nothing is impossible for the Lord!

What does God need in order to release such miracles? Only an available vessel—because every believer can be a carrier of His supernatural power.

6. TO AUTHORIZE US TO BE CUSTODIANS OF THE SUPERNATURAL

Divine encounters also enable us to be custodians of the supernatural. A custodian of the supernatural is someone who holds the keys to the kingdom (see Matthew 16:19); someone who carries the revelation of God, the mysteries of Jesus Christ and of the church. Paul was one such custodian, and he had to face great adversities. (See 2 Corinthians 12:7–10.) If you are a custodian of the supernatural, the spiritual warfare you will engage in will be neither common nor easy. The enemy will always want to bring down and even kill those who carry the revelation and the power from God that can deliver entire peoples, countries, and continents. To be a custodian of the truth, the mysteries, and the supernatural power of God, an encounter with the Holy Spirit is required to activate, empower, and commission us to fulfill this assignment and to enable us to rise above all weaknesses, anxieties, needs, and persecutions.

SEEK GOD'S SUPERNATURAL ENCOUNTERS

Beloved reader, I encourage you to seek God today, to be hungry and thirsty to "go after" supernatural encounters with His Holy Spirit. I believe that to know Christ as Savior is the most beautiful experience that we can have as children of God. And along with our salvation encounter, God wants to give us many more supernatural encounters with His Holy Spirit, in order to empower us, transform us, and lead us to impact nations. As you seek Him, be prepared to have encounters that reflect the various ways the Spirit wants to manifest Himself to you. The Spirit chooses you, but you must make room for Him to invade your life according to His will and purposes.

To receive the Holy Spirit's empowerment and transformation, we must especially keep in mind two things: the need for His anointing, and the need for our surrender to Him.

THE REQUIREMENT OF ANOINTING

We cannot do anything without God's anointing. Remember that Jesus Himself did not enter into His ministry until He was baptized with the Holy Spirit and power. For the first thirty years of His life, Jesus dedicated Himself to the trade of carpentry. It is believed that Joseph, His human father, died when Jesus was a teenager and that He took over the family business at that time. Then, at the age of thirty, He went to the Jordan to be baptized. There He had an encounter with the Holy Spirit where God the Father acknowledged Him publicly, confirmed His calling, anointed Him, and sent Him into ministry full-time.

At the Jordan, John the Baptist testified about Jesus, saying,

I saw the Spirit descending from heaven like a dove, and He remained upon Him. I did not know Him, but He who sent me to baptize with water said to me, "Upon whom you see the Spirit descending, and remaining on Him, this is He who baptizes with the Holy Spirit." And I have seen and testified that this is the Son of God.
(John 1:32–34)

The power of the Holy Spirit that we receive is the same power that operated in the life of the Messiah; when Jesus ascended to heaven, the Father sent His Spirit to empower the church, enabling believers to proclaim the gospel of the kingdom with accompanying signs and wonders. Today, many people leap into ministry without having experienced a transformational divine encounter. They do not know the Holy Spirit and His revelation! They may have some intellectual knowledge of Him, but they lack the power of God in their lives. There are churches today where the leaders are discouraged, but instead of following the principles in this chapter, they try to conduct their ministries in their own strength. That's suicide! True ministry cannot be developed or carried out through our natural abilities. We need the power of God, which comes only through an encounter with the Holy Spirit.

The Holy Spirit does not turn into a different person when He comes to live within us. He has the same potential and presence that He had when He dwelled in Jesus Christ while the Son of God lived on earth. In fact, He is always ready to demonstrate His works and to move in and through us to heal the sick, to cast out demons, and to do other great works. Today, as a child of God, you are a candidate to be used by Him in supernatural power! However, your traditional knowledge and methods must yield to His power and anointing.

Moses had been trained and educated in Pharaoh's court, in all the sciences and wisdom of the Egyptians. (See Acts 7:22.) The Egyptian culture, one of the oldest known today, was very prominent and advanced for its time. Yet it wasn't cultural sophistication or knowledge of the Egyptian war arts that led Moses to become the liberator of Israel; rather, it was the experience he had with the burning bush—the manifestation of the Spirit of God on the summit of Mount Sinai. Moses had left Egypt decades earlier as a murderer, but after his supernatural encounter with the fire of God, he returned to the court of Pharaoh with powerful signs to bend the hard heart of the Egyptian ruler.

Moses risked his life going before the presence of Pharaoh, but he did so because he had returned from the desert empowered and emboldened; what had changed him was the knowledge that he was a representative of the Lord of Hosts. Today, God wants to make you a liberator for your family, your neighborhood, your city, and your nation as His representative. Only an encounter with the Holy Spirit can anoint you to succeed in this. If you will allow God to impact your life, He will take you beyond the traditional methods of ministry you are familiar with; He will enable you to manifest His supernatural power in the natural world and to take dominion over creation with miracles that demonstrate His love and power.

THE REQUIREMENT OF SURRENDER

As we seek divine encounters with the Holy Spirit, we must always remember that surrender is a prerequisite of the anointing, and that Jesus is our model in this. Because Jesus came to earth as a man, to live and die as a representative of the human race on our behalf, it was not legal in a spiritual sense for Him to use His divine glory and majesty among us. He was both fully God and fully man, but at His baptism, He surrendered His life to God the Father and died to Himself. The Jordan was the place where Jesus yielded His right to use the powers of almighty God, and rose up to teach and minister only as a man, in the power of the Holy Spirit. He stripped Himself of His heavenly splendor, of all His divine authority (though not His divine nature); He emptied Himself and started life on earth from scratch as a human being, giving Himself fully to the Holy Spirit.

Likewise, the apostles died to themselves and yielded to the Holy Spirit before being baptized with His power. They established surrender and anointing as their model of action for ministry. (See, for example, Acts 1:12–14; 2:1–4; 4:24–31; 16:25–26.) In the same way, for us to have encounters with the Spirit of God, we must die to self, surrendering to the one true God. Again, Jesus Christ became man to show us the way to the Father. And that way was to die to Himself and be filled with the Spirit, just like any other man or woman needs to do and be. He completed His assignment on earth in the same way and with the same power that any of us can do today. He had to depend fully on the Holy Spirit so that the Father could be revealed through Him, and so that He could remain obedient to God. Only in the power of the Spirit could He overcome the severe temptations and fierce attacks of the enemy, and release the power of God in His generation.

Before Jesus' encounter at His baptism, I don't believe He had ever been tempted or confronted by the devil. But once He had that first encounter with the Spirit of God, He received the power He needed to face and defeat the enemy. Therefore, I believe that until we, too, have a genuine encounter with the Spirit of God, we are not ready to overcome temptation or the flesh, or to engage in spiritual warfare. After we have an encounter with the Spirit, the first thing the enemy does is tempt us, in order to try to steal the fruit of that encounter. We cannot fight such battles in our own strength; it takes the Holy Spirit's help to defeat the enemy and his infernal hosts or to resist the fleshly nature.

If Jesus, being holy and without sin, needed to have an encounter with the Holy Spirit, how much more do we? Thus, wherever God sends us, we have to go, but only after we have surrendered ourselves to the Father, encountered the Holy Spirit, and been empowered by Him.

> **Jesus' encounter with the Holy Spirit at His baptism empowered Him to carry out His assignment on the earth.**

ALLOW THE SPIRIT FREEDOM TO MOVE IN YOUR LIFE

As we have seen, many people in the church have been content merely to be born again and to have the Holy Spirit live inside them; they have failed to seek His power through a supernatural encounter in which they are empowered to do the works of Jesus Christ on earth. If you are a leader in the church, do not pretend to run a supernatural ministry using your natural abilities! That is not the principle that Jesus Christ entrusted to us.

We can have the same relationship that Jesus had with the Spirit of God. However, we cannot reduce this relationship to simple emotion; nor can we confine the Spirit of God within our own ideas or particular denominations. He is too big for that. Let us give Him the freedom to move in us and through us. The Holy Spirit is the steward of the affairs of the kingdom of God on earth; without His presence and power, we cannot represent God in the world.

We must be convinced that God wants us to have an encounter with the person of the Holy Spirit—right now. I urge all believers, as members of the body of Christ, to prepare to experience supernatural encounters—as did Jesus, Paul, and the rest of Christ's apostles. Go to the "Jordan," that place of submission, surrender, and death to self; give up everything, and receive the Holy Spirit and His power.

There is no other option! We need an encounter with the Father to affirm our identity as His children, an encounter with the Son to appropriate the finished work of the cross, and an encounter with the Holy Spirit to be empowered to do the work that has been assigned to us. Today, let us welcome the Spirit who clothes us in power. (See Luke 24:49 NIV.) He is now coming forth, stirring His supernatural power within you so that you can do the works that Jesus did. After having an encounter with the Holy Spirit and walking under His power and authority, your expectation must be that the sick will be healed, that demons will flee when you rebuke them, and that signs and wonders will be manifested to demonstrate the Father's majesty, love, and mercy!

ACTIVATION

If you have never before received Jesus as your Savior, pray with me now:

Heavenly Father, I acknowledge that I am a sinner, and that my sin separates me from You. Today I believe with my heart and confess with my mouth that Jesus is the Son of God, that He died for me on the cross, and that You raised Him from the dead. I repent of all my sins and ask that You forgive me. Jesus, I renounce every covenant with the world, with the flesh, and with the devil, and make a new covenant with You, to love and serve You every day of my life. Enter into my heart and change my life; and if I die today, when I open my eyes I know I'll be in Your arms. Amen!

If you have never before been baptized with the Holy Spirit, with the evidence of speaking in other tongues, raise your hands to God. Let His Spirit begin to fill you; open your mouth and utter the first sounds that come to you. I declare that you are baptized in the Holy Spirit, right now; be immersed in the waters of the Spirit, starting from the bottom of your feet, until you are completely submerged. Begin to swim in those waters. Jesus promised us, *"If you then, being evil, know how to give good gifts to your children, how much more will your heavenly Father give the Holy Spirit to those who ask Him!"* (Luke 11:13).

Now, ask Jesus for an encounter with the Holy Spirit and be filled with His fire.

Dear Jesus, thank You for letting me know You as my personal Lord and Savior, and for baptizing me with Your Holy Spirit. As I read the rest of this book, I ask You to reveal to me the person of the Holy Spirit and give me a supernatural encounter with Him. I want to be empowered and activated in the supernatural to be Your witness here on earth.

Holy Spirit, I surrender my will, my heart, my mind, and my emotions to You so that You may fill all of my being. I renounce the works of the flesh; I renounce the sinful nature. Change me and transform my heart. Break the patterns and cycles of bad habits in my life that prevent me from having an encounter with You. Purify the motivations and intentions of my heart, and establish Your holiness in me. I die to myself, crucifying my flesh, so that You will become more real to me than anything else. I cry out to You, Spirit of God, so that You may make Jesus

Christ real in me; so that You may make the Father real in me; so that you may make the Word of God real in me. I ask You to move in and through me, just as You moved over the face of the waters in the beginning when the world was created.

Holy Spirit, make me a carrier of the power and glory of the Father; make me a custodian of the supernatural, to perform miracles, signs, and wonders in Jesus' name wherever I go, and to make Christ real in people's lives. Reveal Yourself in my life and empower me to fulfill my assignment on earth. I welcome You and I recognize Your presence. Fill me, Holy Spirit!

As I write this, I feel the presence of the Spirit of God. I declare that the words in this book are fulfilled over the life of each reader. Holy Spirit, I ask that every person who reads this book will have a supernatural encounter with You. Amen!

2

WHO IS THE PERSON OF THE HOLY SPIRIT?

I wrote this book because I have a passion for people to have divine encounters with the Holy Spirit and to receive everything God has for them. In order for this to happen, we must know who the Spirit is and how we are meant to relate to Him. There are misconceptions about the Holy Spirit in a number of Christian circles today. Many preachers have taught incorrect doctrine about the Spirit, leading believers in their churches to adopt erroneous thinking, resulting in a poor relationship with the Spirit. Tragically, because of their misconceptions and lack of knowledge, many of these believers are rejecting the Holy Spirit's work in their lives.

Thus, I dedicate this chapter to your getting to know the third person of the Trinity in a new way. We will explore who He is, how He thinks, what His characteristics are, and how He specializes in manifesting God's power. In the next chapter, we will talk about His purpose and assignment on earth.

To begin, it will be helpful to clear up various doubts, mistaken beliefs, and false concepts about the Holy Spirit that have developed in the church over the centuries, many of which we have accepted without realizing it.

When we speak about the Holy Spirit, various questions come to our minds, such as: "What or who is the Holy Spirit?" "What is He like?" "What does He mean to me?" In order to truly know Him and experience His virtues, gifts, and power, we need to destroy any mental strongholds against Him that keep us from perceiving the truth.

WHO THE HOLY SPIRIT IS *NOT*

First, let us establish who the Holy Spirit is *not*. He is not a thing, an element, or any of the following concepts:

+ The Holy Spirit is not a force, although He is powerful.

+ The Holy Spirit is not an emotion, although He comforts us and gives us peace; He has a sensitive nature and feels emotions.

+ The Holy Spirit is not a thought, although He brings to our minds what Jesus has said.

+ The Holy Spirit is not a message, although He comes to reveal messages from heaven.

+ The Holy Spirit is not a dove, although He is soft and tender toward us, like a dove.

+ The Holy Spirit is not wind, although He moves like the wind, unseen but making visible manifestations on physical, emotional, and spiritual environments. We cannot see Him with our natural eyes, but we can feel and experience His presence.

+ The Holy Spirit is not water, although He quenches our spiritual thirst, like water quenches our physical thirst.

+ The Holy Spirit is not fire, although He burns and purifies us like fire burns and purifies physical material. When He comes upon us, He burns all sin, iniquity, and sickness, and He sets us apart to serve the Lord.

Unfortunately, in the minds of many ministers and other Christians, the Holy Spirit has been reduced to some of the concepts mentioned above, which describe aspects of His attributes but are not His *essence*. As a result, the Spirit has been quenched in countless churches, as well as in the lives of many individual believers. For over two thousand years, the church has been tempted to hide or replace the Holy Spirit and the work He carries out on the earth. This is a very dangerous temptation, because when we give in to it, we commit the same sin that led Adam to reject the revealed, supernatural knowledge of God and to substitute it for what was merely natural. That sin, an attempt to be equal with God, was rooted in pride. Trying to serve God using only human strength has led many people to discard the help of the Holy Spirit. As a result, they are dry, stagnant, and burned out. Although they are still alive and breathing in their physical bodies, they are dead in their spirits.

Three key truths differentiate Christianity from any religion: the cross, the Holy Spirit, and the divine supernatural realm. (Genuine Christianity is not a religion but a relationship with the living God through Christ.) The church was born in the midst of a powerful outpouring of the Holy Spirit, through which the supernatural became the norm. It was the Holy Spirit who characterized the Christian movement of the first century. Miracles, signs, and wonders were not isolated events but were a common part of the lives of the early believers. However, in the course of history, the church fell into an "age of replacements," still prominent today, in which charisma replaced anointing, human abilities replaced power, talent replaced spiritual gifts, and methods, programs, and formulas replaced the guidance and inspiration of the Holy Spirit.

But nothing and no one can substitute for the Holy Spirit in our lives, for He is God in our midst.

> **Nothing and no one can replace the Holy Spirit, for He is God in our midst.**

WHO THE HOLY SPIRIT *IS*

Let us now explore in more detail who the Holy Spirit is, reaffirming and expanding on what we discussed above and in chapter 1:

- The Holy Spirit is God Himself, containing everything from God and extending His kingdom on earth, here and now.

- The Holy Spirit is the third person of the Trinity, which consists of God the Father, God the Son, and God the Spirit.

- The Holy Spirit is the eternal breath, or life, of God within a believer.

- The Holy Spirit is the administrator of the riches and gifts of the Lord Jesus.

- The Holy Spirit is to us what Jesus was to His disciples; as the Helper whom Jesus sent us, He is *Immanuel*, "God with us."

- The Holy Spirit is the realm of the Spirit and the supernatural power of God.

- The Holy Spirit is a *Person*, with a mind, will, and emotions.

- Throughout the Bible, we see that the Holy Spirit works under different names and exhibits a variety of qualities. Each one of these descriptions helps us to understand His attributes, His characteristics, His movements, His flow, and His identity as the third person of the Trinity. Let us look at some of the most important attributes of the Spirit.

The Holy Spirit is not a thing. He is a Person!

1. HE IS THE SPIRIT OF GOD

First, the Holy Spirit is the essence of God's own life. When He invades an atmosphere, His presence often becomes tangible, shining in the darkness, reviving everything that was dead, bringing order to chaos, and filling every void. Thus, He works in the same way He did at the beginning of creation: *"The earth was without form, and void; and darkness was on the face of the deep. And the Spirit of God was hovering over the face of the waters. Then God said, 'Let there be light'; and there was light"* (Genesis 1:2–3).

2. HE IS THE BREATH OF LIFE

The Hebrew word translated as *"Spirit"* is *ruach*, which has various meanings, including "breath," "violent exhale," "wind," "respiration," "life," "spirit," and "Spirit." The Holy Spirit is the breath of almighty God, operating on the earth to continue the ministry begun by God the Son, Jesus Christ.

When man was first formed by God from the dust of the earth, his body remained motionless and his mind unthinking until God breathed the breath of life into him; it was only then that he became a living being. (See Genesis 2:7.) Adam was the first person to receive the breath of God—the first to be filled with the Spirit—and he came into existence as a person after that moment. This demonstrates that human beings are nothing without God's Spirit—we are just a piece of earthly matter.

The Holy Spirit is the One who breathes God's life into us. Psalm 33:6 says, *"By the word of the LORD the heavens were made, and all the host of them by the breath of His mouth."* Thus, again, we see that God creates, but the breath of the Almighty is what gives life.

In the Spirit, everything is connected to new life; that is why we can say that we have been *"born again"* by the work of His hand and that we have life in the Spirit. (See John 3:3–8.) Jesus said, *"I have come that they may have life, and that they may have it more abundantly"* (John 10:10). If you are not filled with the Spirit, you do not have the abundant life of Christ. In fact, without the life of the Spirit, it is impossible to please God. (See Romans 8:7–9.) Even if we call ourselves Christians, the truth is that we are not of God without the Spirit because the Scripture says, *"For as many as are led by the Spirit of God, these are sons of God"* (Romans 8:14).

God wants to give you abundant life, where you have more of Him and less of you.

When the breath of God touches a person, everything changes, because His abundant life is working in that individual. Yenny González is a woman from Venezuela, South America, who had been left hopeless by the doctors. Her testimony shows us how the Holy Spirit transformed her life completely—against all odds of medical science.

"For over two decades, I suffered seizures; and for twelve years, I remained mostly bedridden, moving around only by using a wheelchair. Due to poor medical practice, I had been left unable to walk, with my head bent to one side. Ten doctors had basically kicked me out; there was nothing they could do for me. I could scarcely speak for eight years. I found it very difficult to eat and could barely drink. One of the doctors told me that only one side of my head was alive because my neural system was dying, and he said I would not live long.

"Then I began to watch the TBN-Enlace TV station and saw Apostle Maldonado being used by God to work miracles. I started to trust in God and asked Him to heal me, and there my healing began. One day, the Lord told me to make a prophetic statement, and I answered Him, 'God, but how, if I can hardly speak?' So He led me to the prophecy of the dry bones, and, through Apostle Maldonado, taught me about the power of the resurrection.

"When I found out that the Apostle was coming to Venezuela, I asked my family to take me to the Poliedro de Caracas arena, where his meetings were being held. When I got there, everyone witnessed that my head was twisted to one side, and that my uncontrollable shaking was not letting me be in peace. I was already prepared to leave because I was so tired, but I told God, 'Lord, I am not leaving here without my miracle!' It had been a huge effort to travel the three hours from Valencia to Caracas, the capital, but I refused to leave in the same condition in which I had arrived.

"When I heard the Apostle declare healing, I said, 'This is for me!' Little by little, I started to get up from the wheelchair, and then I began to take short steps. As I did this, my legs grew stronger, and I was able to walk to the altar. Now I am alive! The left part of my head had been dead, but the Lord restored the hypothalamus and gave it life. For twelve years, I could not walk without help, but now I can run on my own. I can raise my head high and move around, for the glory and honor of God. Whereas before, eating had been a torture, I can now eat without problems. I never stopped believing in the power of God! I am a testimony that Jesus lives, and of His Holy Spirit who raised me up and gave me a new life."

> **The Holy Spirit is the breath of God and has the power to change us.**

We all need the breath of God today—in our bodies, finances, marriages, ministries, and all other areas. You need the Holy Spirit in every part of your life.

Like Yenny, it doesn't matter what illness you have been diagnosed with, or what medical science says about it. It doesn't matter what financial or relational issues you are facing. Today, the Holy Spirit has a word from God for you, in the now. That word is life and not death, wealth and not poverty, joy and not sadness. God is ready to give you a new life of abundance! Receive it in the name of Jesus. That is the life that the breath of God imparts upon you today.

We cannot know the spiritual realm from the outside; that realm is within us when we are born again and baptized in the Spirit. When the person of the Holy Spirit rests upon us, He is no longer something "foreign" to us. He creates an atmosphere, an environment, where the presence of God dwells, and He gives us life. In the same way that our physical bodies need oxygen to breathe, and fish require water to survive, so the Holy Spirit is necessary for us to exist as "new creatures" in Christ. He is the atmosphere that sustains our lives. When we are born again, the Holy Spirit brings life to our spiritual environment, and this spreads to every area of our existence. In Him, we are raised up by the breath of life from the Almighty!

3. HE IS HOLY

Third, the Spirit is holy. *Holy* means "separate, unique, uncontaminated, and set apart." The Father is holy in His essence, which means that His Spirit is holy in His essential nature as well. Holiness is evident in everything that involves the divine breath. For example, when a person accepts Jesus Christ, is born again, and is baptized in the Holy Spirit, this causes a hunger for holiness to arise in them and leads them to submit to the process of sanctification by the Spirit, through which they increasingly become more like Jesus. As Peter wrote, *"But as He who called you is holy, you also be holy in all your conduct, because it is written, 'Be holy, for I am holy'"* (1 Peter 1:15–16).

Everything the Holy Spirit touches gains life.

4. HE IS SENSITIVE

Fourth, the Holy Spirit is sensitive. It is very important to understand this aspect of His nature. As I described earlier, He is a Person and, as such, has emotions. We must be careful how we develop our relationship with Him, so that it can be a good, healthy, and growing relationship, bearing the fruits of His presence inside us.

The Spirit's character is one of humility and servanthood, helping us to reach the abundant and victorious life that is ours in Christ. Such is the humble nature of the Holy Spirit's work of love and service that the Father does not accept His being insulted. In fact, Jesus said, *"Therefore I say to you, every sin and blasphemy will be forgiven men, but the blasphemy against the Spirit will not be forgiven men"* (Matthew 12:31). To blaspheme the Spirit is to intentionally curse or dishonor Him. This includes attributing evil to the Lord, or denying good things that come from Him. We blaspheme the Holy Spirit when we give the devil and his demons the glory for works that Jesus does. Ultimately, to blaspheme against the

Spirit is to harden one's heart against Him so that we cannot receive the revelation of grace that He extends to us.

We really need to bring the Spirit's supernatural power to our lives, so we cannot behave foolishly with Him. Because of the sensitive nature of the Holy Spirit, there are three things that we must know in order not to offend Him or lose His presence and power: He can be grieved, quenched, and angered.

THE SPIRIT CAN BE GRIEVED

The Word of God warns, *"And do not grieve the Holy Spirit of God…"* (Ephesians 4:30). The Greek word translated *"grieve"* is *lupeo*, which also indicates "afflict, sadden, or hurt." This means that when we grieve the Holy Spirit, we displease and sadden God. As people in the process of consecration, our character still holds many areas that offend the Spirit of God and must be addressed. Ephesians 4:25–32 shows us the attitudes He dislikes: lying, anger, evil words, bitterness, selfish motives, unforgiveness, wicked thoughts, and more.

> **To grieve the Holy Spirit is to literally displease, reject, and sadden God.**

When the Spirit of God is grieved, He will not work inside us. This means that the transformation process in our heart is paralyzed, since everything depends on our communion with Him. We grieve the Spirit of God when we live like unbelievers; when we freely give in to the nature of sin; when we lie, are boastful, steal, curse, become bitter, do not forgive, or fall into sexual immorality. (See Ephesians 4:17–19, 22–29,

31–32; 5:3–5.) If we do these things, the Holy Spirit will not work in us to change our character.

THE SPIRIT CAN BE QUENCHED

"Do not quench the Spirit. Do not despise prophecies" (1 Thessalonians 5:19–20). The Greek word translated *"quench"* is *sbennumi,* meaning "to extinguish." It indicates "to turn off, obstruct the flow, or cut off the source of power." As One who yielded completely to the Spirit, Jesus modeled the way we should live with the Holy Spirit, without hurting or grieving Him.

God has allowed me to travel to many nations, to be in countless churches and ministries, and to meet all kinds of people. As a result, I have seen with my own eyes what it means to grieve and quench the Holy Spirit, and I realize how often we make Him sad with our terrible behavior, lies, and all the other sins I listed above from Ephesians. I regularly see people who don't carry the life of the Spirit with them. How do I know this? Because their faces show it; when I look at them, I don't see any of the joy I would expect, or anything that reflects the presence of the Spirit in them.

Many times, we grieve Him with our plans, limiting His flow so that we can meet our own schedules. Instead of following His guidance, we follow a man-made program and stop Him from expressing Himself freely. For example, using the excuse of preserving "order" in our church services, we put the Holy Spirit in a box and start thinking the church is ours and not God's. That is why we stop following the direction of the Holy Spirit. When we don't give Him room to move and thus abruptly cut His flow, we definitely quench Him.

Many people have no clue as to who the Holy Spirit is, or the way He moves among us. Because of this, when He starts to reveal Himself in a service, the leaders ignore Him and continue with their schedule, instead of giving Him room to manifest and do as He pleases. The Holy Spirit will never flow with our agenda unless it is aligned with the will of God. For this reason, when you hold on to your own plans and suppress the flow of the Spirit of God, what you are really doing is rejecting His personality and His love! You reject the will of God and put a priority on your own selfish motives, obstructing the flow of the Spirit.

> **Grieving the Holy Spirit relates to our character; quenching Him relates to His power.**

THE SPIRIT CAN BE VEXED, OR ANGERED

A third aspect of the Spirit's sensitive nature is that He can be vexed, or angered. *"But [God's people] rebelled, and vexed his Holy Spirit: therefore He was turned to be their enemy, and he fought against them"* (Isaiah 63:10 KJV). Rebelling, hardening one's heart, sinning deliberately, holding on to unforgiveness, and disobeying the will of God—all of these things anger the Holy Spirit. If we push the Spirit of God to this point, He becomes our enemy and fights against us, because rebellion is the spirit of Satan. (See, for example, 1 Samuel 15:23.)

I used to go to a church where the pastor was a very righteous man. He taught me about integrity in finances, how to love people, the importance of a strong family, loyalty, and much more. In fact, He was full of the Spirit; He was baptized in the Holy Spirit and spoke in tongues. However, in the ten years I went to that church, I hardly ever saw demonstrations of the supernatural power of God; there were no miracles, healings, deliverances, or manifestations of the gifts of the Spirit. I thought to myself, *If he is a righteous man, why doesn't the Holy Spirit move here?* One day, after I had already left that church, I asked God the same question. He answered and told me that the power of the Holy Spirit had been quenched, and this displeased God because the pastor did not allow Him to minister miracles or healings among His people.

The Holy Spirit removes His presence from those who anger Him. This is part of the judgment of God.

When we quench and anger the Holy Spirit, we become dry and spiritually dead. If we come to this point, we are content to follow a method, a formula, or a man-made program; we exhibit an appearance of godliness in the church, but the life of the Spirit is nowhere to be found. This shows that if we do not provide an environment where the Holy Spirit can flow, supernatural power will not be present, and miracles will not take place.

5. HE IS THE GIFT OF GOD AND THE GIVER OF GIFTS

Fifth, the Holy Spirit is a supernatural gift, given to us by God's grace as proof of His love, and as the affirmation that we are one with Him in Christ. The Holy Spirit is also the Giver of spiritual gifts. In the Bible, we see that Paul encouraged Timothy, saying, *"I remind you to stir up the gift of God which is in you"* (2 Timothy 1:6). We have to *"stir up the gift of God."* This means that if we allow the precious spiritual gift that God has given us to remain dormant, we run the risk of confusing it with our own talent, reducing it to something natural, ignoring it, or using it for the wrong reasons. Additionally, many Christians seek first the gifts of the Spirit, but it's more important to focus on the *Person* of the Spirit who gives the gifts. Moreover, if we focus on the gifts more than on the Person, we risk falling into false doctrines.

6. HE IS THE SEAL OF GOD AND THE MARK OF HIS APPROVAL

"In [Jesus] you also trusted, after you heard the word of truth, the gospel of your salvation; in whom also, having believed, you were sealed with the

Holy Spirit of promise" (Ephesians 1:13). The Holy Spirit is the Seal of God. That which is sealed with the Spirit of God has His life, characteristics, and virtues. To have the seal of God also means to be backed up by His power; we receive His approval and support.

> When the Holy Spirit is quenched in a church, the power of God does not flow, and the result is a church without life.

The question we must consider is this: If we deny the Spirit by our unbelief, how can we be sealed by Him? For example, if an individual or ministry denies the move of the Holy Spirit, who will back them up in their endeavors? The truth is that no revival will come over a congregation or territory until the leaders and people acknowledge the Spirit of God, because that would be spiritually illegal; the seal of approval from heaven would be missing.

Nowadays, the church as a whole has lost its passion to seek God's approval. But as the body of Christ, we *must* demonstrate the power of God—especially when we face witchcraft, idolatry, and other forces of darkness—and that power must be visible to all. That is why the following testimony from Pastor Samson Samuel, from the Holy Agni church in India, is not just another story. It is proof of what can happen when we walk in the Holy Spirit with heaven's seal of approval.

"My wife and I had been ordained pastors for many years, but we knew there was more of God—and we needed it. We wanted to see the miracles, signs, and wonders that Jesus performed on earth manifested today. In our desperation, early one morning, we cried out to the Lord to lead us to the spiritual father who could help us, and suddenly the King Jesus Ministry website popped up on our laptop.

"Until that moment, we didn't know anything about King Jesus Ministry or Apostle Maldonado, but as we looked through the website, the presence of God fell upon us, and we had a beautiful encounter with the Holy Spirit. Immediately, we knew that this was the divine connection we were looking for and that we were being empowered to move in the supernatural. The question now was where to start. In India, anything supernatural is usually in the realm of witchcraft rather than the realm of the Holy Spirit, so we started to watch Apostle's preachings online, purchasing his books, and even following him on social media; we were hungry for what he carried from God. When we came in contact with Apostle Maldonado, not only did we receive his spiritual fatherhood, but we were also activated to walk in the divine supernatural and to flow in miracles with faith and boldness.

"One Sunday during our church service, we saw a powerful change take place. Our church had an encounter with the love and power of God! That day, after hearing preaching about the power of the cross, a Hindu woman asked for us to pray for her because she had been sick for years and had pains throughout her body. When we prayed for the woman, she started to manifest signs that the Holy Spirit was moving on her, and she fell under the power of God. I rebuked the demon that tormented her, we prayed for her to receive Jesus, and she was completely set free.

"After this, she was left in awe regarding what she had seen God do in her, and she asked if we could also pray for a family member who was paralyzed from the waist down due to an accident. She told us that this relative had metal screws and rods in her body to support her bones. In front of everyone, I called her paralyzed family member using my cell phone and declared healing over her body. Then I heard the Holy Spirit tell me that this woman had one leg shorter than the other as a result of the surgery she'd had. I told her what I heard, and suddenly, we heard a cry of joy through the cell phone because she had started walking. Everyone there glorified the Lord! Later, many people testified of hearing Jesus speak to them, and now they know that He is the true and living God.

"Ever since that day, our ministry has experienced the power of God with miracles, signs, wonders, healings, and deliverances. We have a spiritual father—a spiritual authority to whom we hold ourselves accountable—and we walk under that covering. But above all, the Holy Spirit has placed His seal over us, and now we are walking in the supernatural!"

We receive many testimonies like this one from every corner of the earth. It's sad that some people think God's approval depends on the size of their church building rather than on the seal of His Spirit. Today, people call "the church of the Lord" any place where a large congregation meets, and they think that the greater the numbers, the more legitimacy God gives that church. However, the requirement for a church to receive God's approval is giving the Holy Spirit the freedom to move, and allowing themselves to be led by Him. Many churches can look, sound, and even act like they are living in obedience to God, but we cannot confuse these appearances and activities with the seal of approval from the Holy Spirit.

7. HE IS THE TANGIBLE PROOF OF GOD'S PRESENCE IN US AND AMONG US

The Holy Spirit is also the tangible proof of God's presence. When the Holy Spirit dwells within us, He manifests the presence of God, for that presence is contained in Him, and the Spirit reveals to us the Father and the Son. Every born-again Christian has the life of the Spirit inside them, and should be able to see and feel the manifestation of the presence of the Lord. A lack of spiritual activity in a person's life is a sign that there is no presence of God or movement from heaven in their being. Likewise, when the presence of God is not felt in a church, it means that the Holy Spirit is absent; His life does not flow there. But when the Holy Spirit enters an atmosphere, He controls the manifestation of the presence of God that wants to move in that place; it is then that we can demonstrate, impart, and loosen His grace and supernatural power to heal, deliver, prosper, and restore people in God.

> **The Holy Spirit controls the presence of God—He is the One who displays and manifests that presence.**

THE HOLY SPIRIT SPECIALIZES IN MANIFESTING THE POWER OF GOD!

To conclude this chapter on the person of the Holy Spirit, I want to stress that there are aspects of God in which the Spirit specializes, and one of them is His power. In fact, we cannot talk about the Holy Spirit without speaking of His power. When the church was formed, the emphasis was on the power of the Holy Spirit to save, deliver, heal, and do signs and wonders—everything with the goal of confirming the preaching of the gospel. Jesus said to His disciples, *"You shall receive power when the Holy Spirit has come upon you; and you shall be witnesses to Me in Jerusalem, and in all Judea and Samaria, and to the end of the earth"* (Acts 1:8). And that is exactly what happened in the early church.

Nowadays, we need to return to the manifestations of the Holy Spirit that gave rise to the early church. If the vessels—we, the disciples of Jesus—are clean and available, then the Holy Spirit will use us to manifest His power. But if we don't allow His power to flow, we quench Him.

Are you quenching the Holy Spirit in any area of your life? Is He quenched in your home or ministry? Have you done something that upsets Him? Are you still holding on to something you need to give up, instead of surrendering it to Him? Is there anything you're doing that is turning off the power of God? Please join me in the following prayers, so that nothing will hinder you from knowing, loving, and being filled with the person of the Holy Spirit.

> **Every time the life of the Spirit is present in a child of God, power will flow.**

ACTIVATION

1. Repent for having grieved, quenched, or angered the Spirit of God. Repeat this prayer out loud:

Heavenly Father, I ask that You would show me the areas where I have grieved and quenched You. I repent with all my heart, recognizing that I need the Holy Spirit more than the air I breathe, and asking for everything that is dead inside me to be brought to life by the fire of Your presence. May Your breath of life fall upon every one of those dead areas, and may I be changed forever. I pray this in the name of Jesus, believing that You are working in me. Amen.

2. There are many leaders in the church who have quenched, grieved, and rejected the power of God, allowing human substitutes as replacements, instead of welcoming the Spirit of God and letting Him move freely among their congregations. If you are a leader and your church is dry, with no miracles, healings, breakthroughs, or other moves of the Spirit, you need to repent. These are all signs that the Spirit of God has been quenched. Repent now!

3. Ask the Father to breathe His life and Spirit upon you, so that you may have intimate communion with Him. I pray that you will receive the breath of God. In the name of Jesus, receive His abundant life now!

THE PURPOSE AND ASSIGNMENT
OF THE SPIRIT

Now that we have learned more about who the Holy Spirit is, let us look further into His purpose and assignment on earth. The Spirit remains in constant activity because His work in our present world will be finished only when Christ returns for His bride; His work is intimately related to the church on earth. (See Revelation 22:17.) After Jesus ascended to heaven following His resurrection, the Father sent the Holy Spirit to earth to fulfill a new assignment consisting of empowering those who would believe in Jesus to be His witnesses, and to equip them to demonstrate the supernatural through miracles, signs, and wonders, just as Christ did. The same Spirit who dwelled in Jesus would dwell in everyone who confessed Jesus as Lord and Savior; the Spirit would reveal the Father to them and guide them into all truth.

We have seen that as Christ's younger siblings, washed by His blood and justified by His sacrifice, we are co-heirs with Him (see Romans 8:17) and have the same potential to be instruments of God on earth that He had. The Holy Spirit who breathed life into Adam at the beginning of creation and later anointed, empowered, and raised Jesus from the dead is the same Spirit who now breathes upon us. The Spirit who rested upon the one hundred and twenty people in the Upper Room at Pentecost and baptized with fire all who were waiting for the Lord's promise is the same Holy Spirit who now rests upon the body of Christ—the church—ready to continually baptize with fire all who will receive the Lord's promise today.

It is essential for us to understand that the Holy Spirit's assignment cannot be completed without the church's participation, and that the church's assignment cannot be completed without the ever-present help of the Holy Spirit. The problem of fulfilling the Holy Spirit's assignment lies with the church, because of our limited understanding of His purpose and functions.

> **The key to understanding the Holy Spirit is knowing His purposes, assignment, and functions on earth.**

Let us look at some of the most important ways the Holy Spirit works in the church and in our lives as believers.

1. HE REVEALS TO US THE FULLNESS OF THE PERSON OF JESUS

The Holy Spirit knows Jesus completely, and His function among us is to reveal everything about Jesus' person, character, mind, and love, as well as the nearness of His second coming. Accordingly, the apostle Paul prayed to the Father for the Ephesians...

> *That He would grant you, according to the riches of His glory, to be strengthened with might through His Spirit in the inner man, that Christ may dwell in your hearts through faith; that you, being rooted and grounded in love, may be able to comprehend with all the saints what is the width and length and depth and height...[of] the love of Christ.* (Ephesians 3:16–19)

The Holy Spirit's leadership is supernatural. Without Him, it is impossible for us to know Jesus and to be filled with His love. We cannot understand Him through our reason or through any of our five senses; our natural intuition is not of much use, either. Even the disciples of Jesus, who lived with Him day and night, were unable to see Him as He really was until the Father sent them the help of the Spirit of God. (See, for example, Matthew 16:17.)

Thus, we need the Holy Spirit's revelation of the person of the Savior. That is why Jesus said about the Spirit, *"He will glorify Me, for He will take of what is Mine and declare it to you"* (John 16:14). Without the Holy Spirit, there can be no revelation of Jesus and no understanding of those spiritual things that remain mysterious to humanity.

2. HE REVEALS TO US THE FINISHED WORK OF THE CROSS

In the Hebrew culture of the Old Testament, the truth was established by witnesses. We know that Jesus fulfilled all of the law, which is why the Holy Spirit was assigned to be a witness of His life and work on earth. This Spirit is the only One who was present from the beginning to the end of Jesus' human life—and beyond that to His resurrection. (See, for example, Luke 1:35; Matthew 3:16; Luke 23:46; Hebrews 9:14; Romans 8:11.) However, the church has not fully understood the finished work of Jesus, nor the price that was paid on the cross: Christ bore all of our sins, curses, sicknesses, and failures, and He overcame death!

If the Holy Spirit does not reveal Jesus to us, we cannot know Him.

At the cross, there was a divine exchange. Everything that humanity deserved because of its disobedience and rebellion was put upon Jesus, and everything that Jesus deserved because of His full obedience was given to those who believe in Him. He took our sin so that we would receive His forgiveness and salvation. Although the Word tells us about this, we would not be able to fully understand this exchange if the Holy Spirit did not reveal it to us. Where does this revelation begin? The very moment we sincerely ask, *"What will a man give in exchange for his soul?"* (Mark 8:37)—in other words, when we acknowledge to God that there is nothing we can do to redeem ourselves. I believe that centuries earlier, David had a revelation of this truth, which is why he said, *"What is man that You are mindful of him, and the son of man that You visit him?"* (Psalm 8:4).

When we have a revelation of the finished work of Jesus on the cross, the Holy Spirit also gives us the conviction that He took our sicknesses so that we would receive His healing; He took our slavery so that we would receive His freedom; He took our poverty so that we would receive His prosperity; He took our shame so that we would receive His glory; He took our death so that we would receive His life.

It is important for Christians to have this full revelation of the work that Jesus finished on the cross. Many people consider what Jesus accomplished through His death to be a legend, not something that can have a transforming effect on their lives. To avoid the trap of this kind of thinking, we should pursue God's revelation from this day forward. Without it, we will live in ignorance, darkness, and deception regarding spiritual truth; and when that occurs, the enemy will begin to build strongholds in our minds.

The Holy Spirit is the Agent in charge of revealing the truth to us; He is the One who brings divine knowledge so that we can come out of spiritual darkness. He guides us into all truth and leads us out of ignorance concerning the work of the cross. In fact, the Holy Spirit has been revealing the reality of the cross and the resurrection for over two thousand years. He has done so from generation to generation so that people would come to know Christ and the will of God for their lives, so they would stop doubting that Jesus wants to—and is able to—heal, deliver, and bring prosperity to every person who believes in Him.

The enemy knows that if Christians are ignorant about what Jesus paid for on the cross, they will never be able to claim what belongs to them. Therefore, if you still doubt that the will of God is to save, heal, deliver, prosper, and transform you, go to the Holy Spirit, and He will reveal it to you. When you truly know and receive the truth, you will walk in the power of the finished work of Jesus and be able to appropriate all the benefits of the cross I have just described, including freedom, healing, and restoration. In this way, walking in the supernatural works of God will become the norm for you.

Everything you need at this very moment, Jesus has already provided at the cross, and the Holy Spirit reveals this truth to you—now! If you are sick, I declare healing over your body. If you are afflicted in your mind, I declare deliverance and peace. If your finances are stagnant, I break the spirit of poverty off your life today and release the riches that Jesus has already given us. The moment the Holy Spirit reveals to you what Jesus has already paid for at the cross, you will be free. You will never again live in spiritual ignorance or walk in darkness. The enemy has wanted to keep you ignorant for a long time, but I assure you that the will of God is for you to be healed, prosperous, transformed, and renewed. Above all, He wants your entire family to be saved. Receive it now, in the name of Jesus!

3. HE REVEALS TO US SATAN'S DEFEAT AT THE CROSS

Jesus said of the Holy Spirit, *"And when He has come, He will convict the world of sin,...and of judgment:...because the ruler of this world is judged"* (John 16:8, 11). Only the Holy Spirit can reveal to us how Jesus defeated Satan, because the Spirit was there as a witness, and because Jesus disarmed the devil and dethroned him in a supernatural way. The Spirit shows us that Christ dealt the enemy an absolute, definitive, irrevocable, and eternal defeat.

Satan hates it when we speak the truth about the cross, because the cross is the point of reference for both his conquest and the salvation of man. The cross is where he lost his dominion and power over human beings. (See, for example, Colossians 2:15.) If you are facing problems—fear, doubt, confusion, trials, tribulations, crises—if you are being persecuted, or if the enemy is attacking your body, mind, or spirit, cry out to God's Spirit and say, "Holy Spirit, reveal to me Satan's total defeat by Christ." Then prepare to apply Jesus' victory to your situation.

Why is it so important for us to understand Satan's defeat? Because when Satan's current state is revealed to us, we understand that we have power and authority in Christ to destroy his works. The enemy is conquered. Jesus defeated him! However, we must take authority over Satan and all his powers of darkness to enforce that victory. Keep in mind that the power and authority to destroy the works of the devil will be active in us as long as we obey God and live in intimate relationship with Him. Let's establish the victory that Jesus has already won at the cross!

Jesus defeated Satan at the cross; since then, the state of the enemy is that he is defeated, dethroned, destroyed, and disarmed.

How do we demonstrate that Satan has been defeated? By worshipping God, and then by manifesting His works. That is why, when I held a Supernatural Encounter conference in Los Angeles, California, I asked the four thousand people in attendance who were desperate to have an encounter with the Holy Spirit to first worship God. Next, I told them that a wave of creative miracles would come upon all of them. The moment I declared this, the atmosphere changed, and hundreds of testimonies of miracles were documented. However, three of them caught my attention in a powerful way.

A man named Abel testified, "I was still a child when the primary function of my kidneys began to deteriorate due to an infection. However, it wasn't until a year ago that I began to retain a large amount of liquid. The doctor told me that my kidneys had collapsed, and they had to insert an arteriovenous fistula (AVF) to artificially help me urinate.

"At the Supernatural Encounter, after they prayed for me, they challenged my faith and asked me to do what I could not do before. I went to the bathroom and was able to urinate normally! When the doctors examined me, they confirmed that God had created new kidneys in me!"

A woman named Amaris declared, "When I was born, I was diagnosed with tumors in the kidney glands. These two small organs, each located above the kidneys, produce hormones, regulate metabolism, help the response to stress, and control blood pressure. To save my life, the doctors removed my kidney glands when I was only a week old, and put me on medication for the rest of my life. For twenty-six years, I waited for a miracle that never arrived—until the day I went to serve as a volunteer at the Supernatural Encounter: Los Angeles. I was about to begin serving in the cafeteria when the Holy Spirit led me to the auditorium to hear a message. At that very instant, Apostle Maldonado began to declare a wave of creative miracles, and I said, 'The miracle I've been waiting for my entire life is here!' The moment he began to pray, I felt an intense fire in my body and what felt like a hand inside my body pressing right above my kidneys. That day, the Spirit of God created kidney glands in me! Days later, medical exams confirmed that I had in fact received my miracle."

The third testimony was from a man named Andy, who said, "At birth, doctors diagnosed me with hypothyroidism. They told my mother I had only half a thyroid and that because of this, I would have to take Levothyroxine, a hormone replacement pill, for the rest of my life. The pill made me feel lethargic all day; I would easily tire, and my weight fluctuated. Since I was raised attending church, I had heard about the supernatural, but I had never experienced it. Finally, I was fed up with living with an illness that I knew God could cure. I went to the Supernatural Encounter: Los Angeles expecting to receive my miracle. When Apostle said that we should be desperate to have an encounter with the Holy Spirit, I began to cry out, and I asked Him to touch me. Suddenly, as I worshipped, I felt hot and cold sensations in my throat, and I began to shake uncontrollably. When I touched my throat, I felt a slight protrusion that I did not have before. The Holy Spirit had created the part of my thyroid that I had been missing!"

At the cross, Jesus truly conquered sin, sickness, and death! Ask the Holy Spirit to reveal this to you now.

4. HE CONVICTS THE WORLD OF SIN

"And when He has come, He will convict the world of sin…because they do not believe in Me" (John 16:8–9). The term *"world"* here does not refer merely to the planet; rather, it comes from the Greek word *kosmos* and indicates the established system or social order in which human beings live without Christ. The Holy Spirit is in the church revealing Christ, but He is also working in the lives of unbelievers, bringing them conviction of sin, so that they may proceed to salvation. The Bible says that the world, the established system, is not a friend of the truth. Many people don't want to hear the truth, because the spirit of the world and the Spirit of God are always in opposition. Every time we speak the truth of God, we can expect to be persecuted or rejected because in the spiritual realm there is a clash between these two spirits.

No person could come to Jesus except through the Holy Spirit who convicts them of sin. Our job is to preach the truth, so that the Holy Spirit can do His part, with the result that sinners will repent and be saved. The Holy Spirit, who dwells within Christians, brings conviction of sin to believers, too; for although we have been justified by the work of Christ, we sin each time we disobey God, either consciously or unconsciously. Although we are now enemies of sin, sin will continually besiege us while we are on earth. Thus, when the Holy Spirit brings conviction to us concerning some area of our lives, we must make the decision to repent before God, reject and fight against that sin, and change the way we live.

There are things in your life, dear reader, that are not right before God. If you can say, "I feel conviction now," then this is the moment to repent. I have felt the conviction of the Holy Spirit myself and know that if one does not yield, if one does not surrender and obey the Holy Spirit, the heart becomes hardened, and consequences will come later that tend to be even worse.

Let me give you an illustration of how the Holy Spirit works in our lives to convict us. I was speaking with a group of pastors when they suddenly started to talk about another pastor and the things that he was doing wrong. Without realizing it, I began to participate in the conversation because what they were saying was true. Suddenly, I felt a strong conviction inside of me and began to feel bad. I immediately repented and recognized before God that, although what they were saying was true, I did not have the right to judge that other pastor.

That day, I learned that we must be sensitive each time the Holy Spirit brings us conviction regarding something that we are doing wrong. He never condemns us; He only convicts us of sin so we can be restored in our relationship with Him. (See John 3:17.)

Has the Holy Spirit convicted you of sin in some area of your life? Is there perhaps brokenness or even infidelity in your marriage? Have you neglected to give the tithes of your finances to God? Are you in rebellion against your parents? In any area of your life in which the Holy Spirit is bringing you conviction, be sensitive to it; do not hesitate to repent, and God will forgive you, for it is written, *"A broken and a contrite heart— these, O God, You will not despise"* (Psalm 51:17).

> ## The Holy Spirit convicts the world and the unbeliever of sin, but He does not condemn them.

5. HE HELPS US FULFILL OUR ROLES AND RESPONSIBILITIES

The Holy Spirit was designated by the Father and the Son as the official Helper for the roles and responsibilities that God entrusts us with. He collaborates with us in what goes beyond the natural. However, He does not do the work *for* us.

At all times when He was on earth, Jesus ministered with the help of the Holy Spirit, yet Christ did His part. He was a Man of maturity and firm character, who took the responsibility that the Father delegated to Him and fulfilled it completely, working hard in collaboration with the Spirit. In other words, the Spirit of the Lord does the supernatural part, while we must do the natural part. This is the way God and human beings are meant to work together.

When we cry out to the Lord for help, He will send His Holy Spirit to us. Jesus knew this reality, which is why He told His disciples, *"It is to your advantage that I go away; for if I do not go away, the Helper will not come to you; but if I depart, I will send Him to you"* (John 16:7). The *Amplified Bible* enables us to better understand the meaning of the word *Helper* in relation to the Holy Spirit: *"But the Helper (Comforter, Advocate, Intercessor—Counselor, Strengthener, Standby), the Holy Spirit, whom the Father will send in My name..."* (John 14:26).

Day by day, all of us face hardships, make difficult decisions, endure accusations of wrongdoing by the enemy, and experience rejection by other people—and all of this weakens us. In those times, we need help and faith to address what we cannot deal with on our own. We must pray more fervently and seek the assistance of God in everything we do, allowing our Helper to meet our needs.

6. HE COUNSELS US

The Holy Spirit is called the Counselor because in times of affliction, discouragement, anxiety, and hopelessness, He is the One who comforts our hearts with the loving presence of the Father. He came to bring peace to our hearts, to remind us of the promises of God and of our calling and purpose, and to help us overcome all trials.

Erick and Nydia Navas, from West Palm Beach, Florida, came to know the Holy Spirit as the great Counselor when they were in the midst of a marriage crisis. They had to hold on to Him tightly, because stress, depression, a bipolar disorder, autism, and adultery all converged to attack them and their union. This is Nydia's testimony.

"When Erick and I got married, everything was going very well until my husband began to suffer from depression without realizing it. As a result, he started doing things that damaged our relationship. A few years after this, our son Christian was diagnosed with autism, and Erick's depression worsened. Months later, Val, the youngest of our children, was also diagnosed with autism. In addition, my husband started suffering from panic attacks, and twice he tried to commit suicide. The second time, Christian, our nine-year-old, prevented him, and Erick was admitted to a psychiatric ward.

"My husband came out of the hospital diagnosed with bipolarity. He had to take twelve pills a day, and the medication caused him to become like a zombie and fall asleep everywhere. He could not work and did not seem to care about anything. At the same time, Christian started going to therapy for autism. This became an extremely stressful situation for me because I carried all of the family's responsibilities on my shoulders, and I had to take care of my husband and two boys. It was so overwhelming that I wanted to die!

"On top of all this, my husband cheated on me multiple times, and this destroyed what was left of our relationship, to the point that we separated for fourteen months and eventually started the divorce process. Our lives were destroyed and our family was completely broken.

"However, one day, we were invited to King Jesus Ministry. We were empty and numb to all feelings, but from the very first service we attended, the love of God filled our lives. When we went up to the altar, the Holy Spirit convicted us of our sin, and we repented. Just a few days later, we were baptized and began the process of discipleship for new believers. The Lord really worked on us, delivering us from unforgiveness, lack of identity, generational curses, and much more. Today, six months later, my husband does not need to take any more medication, Christian doesn't need therapy, and Val and the others have been diagnosed as completely healthy.

"When we started to meet the Holy Spirit as our Counselor and depend completely upon God, all of the burdens we were carrying were lifted off. Instead of getting a divorce, our marriage was restored, and just a short time ago my husband and I renewed our wedding vows. Our family has also been restored. We all serve in the church, and even our finances are better than ever. Now we are a family that has been transformed by God. When we lived in affliction, discouragement, anxiety, and hopelessness, the Holy Spirit came to us and healed our hearts."

If you are going through tough times that have driven you to walk in stress, if your family life is in danger, if the enemy is attacking your mind to resist the things of God, if your ministry is dry and needs the rivers of the Spirit, the Counselor is ready to help you! What do you have to do? Simply ask, from the bottom of your heart, for Him to help you, and He will come.

THE PURPOSE AND ASSIGNMENT OF THE SPIRIT 75

7. HE INTERCEDES FOR US

Every time we need God's grace, protection, provision, or forgiveness, the Holy Spirit cries out to the Lord and intercedes for us. *"The Spirit also helps in our weaknesses. For we do not know what we should pray for as we ought, but the Spirit Himself makes intercession for us with groanings which cannot be uttered"* (Romans 8:26). The Spirit of the Lord feels the weight of our weaknesses, and He takes our burdens and makes them His own. He goes before the Father and intercedes for God to work in our favor.

The Holy Spirit also prays for us so that the will of God may be done in our lives. We do not always know what that will is, or how to pray about it properly, but the Spirit intercedes for us to carry it out, regardless of any hardships in our way. *"Now He who searches the hearts knows what the mind of the Spirit is, because He makes intercession for the saints according to the will of God"* (Romans 8:27).

8. HE REVEALS THE TRUTH TO US

Jesus said, *"When He, the Spirit of truth, has come, He will guide you into all truth"* (John 16:13). Since one of the names of the Holy Spirit is *"the Spirit of truth,"* we can know that truth is a Person. This reality applies to the full Godhead. The Father has all truth (see, for example, Romans 3:4), and Jesus is called *"the way, the truth, and the life"* (John 14:6). The Spirit is the One who reveals the truth of God to us, and He does it progressively, because God is infinite, vast, eternal, and everlasting. We could never take in all of God's truth at once.

Many people make the mistake of rejecting the Holy Spirit without realizing that they are thereby rejecting God's truth. *"And for this reason God will send them strong delusion, that they should believe the lie, that they all may be condemned who did not believe the truth but had pleasure in unrighteousness"* (2 Thessalonians 2:11–12).

We cannot know ultimate truth without the Holy Spirit. If your heart is sincere in its desire to know the truth concerning God, Jesus, or the Bible, the Holy Spirit will guide you in regard to any question or doubt you may have, because His function is to reveal the truth to the children of God and to alert them to error. This is especially important because Jesus said that one of the signs of the end times would be deception. (See, for example, Matthew 24:3–13, 23–27.) If we understand this danger, we will ask the Holy Spirit to guide us into all truth.

One of the conditions we must meet for the Holy Spirit to fulfill His function of revealing God's truth to us is desiring to know the truth and obey it. Many people seek the truth merely out of curiosity, or to accumulate knowledge, or to demonstrate how wise they are, but they have no intention of obeying it. God doesn't work that way! The Holy Spirit will reveal the truth to you when you desire it because you are hungry for God, and when you are willing to submit to it and obey it.

Because they do not understand the purpose and assignment of the Holy Spirit, many ministers today try to use their personality or charisma as the basis from which to operate in the power of God. They ignore the fact that the real basis of supernatural power is God's truth. When you preach the truth, which is Jesus Christ, the power of the Holy Spirit must manifest itself.

> **People who have an encounter with the Holy Spirit love and long for the truth.**

9. HE TEACHES US "ALL THINGS"

Another function of the Holy Spirit is to teach us everything we need to fulfill our role in God's purposes on earth. Jesus proclaimed, *"But the Helper, the Holy Spirit, whom the Father will send in My name, He will teach you all things, and bring to your remembrance all things that I said to you*" (John 14:26). The Spirit reminds us of the teachings of Jesus, reveals the Word to us, and equips us to operate as children of God.

When the Holy Spirit comes to us, He guides us in regard to the past, He directs us in the present, and He leads us toward the future in a way that no one else can. In other words, by the Holy Spirit, we have the ability to know and understand "*all things*": things that have happened, things that are occurring now, and things that are to come. Therefore, if a believer, through revelation, speaks something that Jesus did and said in His ministry, which may not even have been written about, it will manifest in the now to minister to us today.

To "bring to our remembrance" means to cause us to return in our thoughts to a place, a moment, or a specific time that we have experienced. Accordingly, when I read about events in the Scriptures, I speak and feel as though I myself have been there physically. Although my physical body was never in those places, I experience that sensation because the Holy Spirit dwells in me and He was there, so He can help me remember what happened at every moment. This is one reason why no one can say they know the Holy Spirit or have a relationship with Him and remain unchanged. When the Holy Spirit comes upon us, He transforms us, and in that instant, God begins to reveal to us His mysteries.

God has never wanted to hide anything from us or to become an enigma to us. His original intention was that we would know Him in all of His majesty, omnipresence, omnipotence, glory, dominion, and power. With His death on the cross, Jesus removed our sin and gave us access to know "*all things*"—the same access He had on earth. Jesus has made us co-heirs with Him, and the Father calls us His children. (See Romans 8:17.) You have the same access to revelation that Jesus has! Thus, when the Holy Spirit comes, what had been veiled leaps to light, and God authorizes us to know His mysteries.

Moreover, we are living in times when revelation is being revealed in a greater way. Even human knowledge has increased dramatically in the last century—and so far, in this present one, in a super-accelerated way. We are sure that it will increase even more. Likewise, the mysteries of heaven are being declassified like never before. Things are being revealed to us that the prophets of old never knew. Moses, David, and Abraham could not see spiritually what we are able to see today. Thus, we are part of the generation that God marked when He said that the Holy Spirit would give us the ability to know *"all things."* We must allow God's revelation to take us beyond the limitations of our five physical senses and to expand our spiritual capacities.

> **When the Holy Spirit comes, the supernatural prevails, and revelation takes the place of our five physical senses, thus expanding all our capacities.**

10. HE LEADS AND GUIDES US

Another of the Holy Spirit's functions is to guide and direct us on the right path. In John 16:13, Jesus told His disciples, "[The Spirit] *will guide you into all truth;…and He will tell you things to come."* His guidance is trustworthy because He always exercises it according to the will of the Father and with full knowledge of what is to come. He knows our future; therefore, He knows how to lead us to a good destination.

The Spirit gives us His supernatural guidance through the words of the Bible, prophetic words by other believers, visions, His voice, and other ways. Ultimately, Jesus is the Way by which believers must be led, and the Truth we must reach. (See John 14:6.)

There are Christians who are seeking something physical, material, or human to guide them; however, the Holy Spirit, who lives within us, is the right One to guide us, through our intimate relationship with Him. He leads us from the inside out. In an upcoming chapter, I will describe the different ways He does this. For now, it is enough to know that just as He guided Jesus to the Jordan to be baptized, to the wilderness to be tested, through each step of His ministry on earth, to the cross to die for our sins, and to the resurrection, He now guides us to the place of our assignment, to undertake the right business, to make the right decisions, to offer ourselves as an acceptable sacrifice to God, to renounce the things that do not please the Father, and to do His whole will. We know that the Holy Spirit is continually leading us to the truth. He will never lead us to falsehood or cause us to make mistakes; He will always guide us to correct decisions. Again, the Holy Spirit knows the will of God, so no one is better able than He to guide us on the right path for our lives.

11. HE BEARS WITNESS OF JESUS, AND ENABLES US TO BEAR WITNESS

The Holy Spirit is Jesus' witness on the earth, and He speaks about Him to us. Jesus said, *"There is another who bears witness of Me, and I know that the witness which He witnesses of Me is true"* (John 5:32).

The Spirit of God also bears witness of Jesus through us to other people. John the Baptist testified of Jesus and of reconciliation with the Father through Him. (See, for example, John 1:29.) Jesus' disciples encountered the risen Christ, believed in Him, and became His witnesses after the Spirit came upon them at Pentecost. They declared about Jesus' death and resurrection, *"And we are His witnesses to these things, and so also is the Holy Spirit whom God has given to those who obey Him"* (Acts 5:32). As we have seen, an encounter with the risen Christ transformed Paul, one of the biggest persecutors of the church, so that he went on to become one of the strongest defenders of the faith as he testified about Jesus.

Likewise, every disciple of Christ today must bear witness of Jesus in the power of the Spirit. Jesus said, *"You shall receive power when the Holy Spirit has come upon you; and you shall be witnesses to Me in Jerusalem, and in all Judea and Samaria, and to the end of the earth"* (Acts 1:8). No one can be a witness of Jesus without first having an encounter with Him. And an encounter with Him comes as a result of believing in the redemptive power of the cross and being born again.

12. HE ANOINTS US WITH POWER

We are not witnesses of Christ because of our own qualifications, such as advanced educational degrees, but because we have received the power of the Holy Spirit. At the start of His ministry, Jesus said,

> *The Spirit of the LORD is upon Me, because He has anointed Me to preach the gospel to the poor; He has sent Me to heal the broken-hearted, to proclaim liberty to the captives and recovery of sight to the blind, to set at liberty those who are oppressed.* (Luke 4:18)

The word *anointed* means to be empowered with divine abilities. Thus, to be anointed by God is to be supernaturally endued with an ability to do "impossible" things. Jesus was anointed to heal the sick, to cast out demons, and even to walk upon the water. *"God anointed Jesus of Nazareth with the Holy Spirit and with power, who went about doing good and healing all who were oppressed by the devil, for God was with Him"* (Acts 10:38).

When the Holy Spirit comes upon us in anointing, we are empowered to move in the supernatural with boldness, because that is the nature of our Lord. God transforms us into useful vessels, ready to help with the impossible circumstances of mankind, just as He did with Jesus. The Holy Spirit is always available to supply every physical, emotional, and spiritual need, and He will finish His work on earth through us.

The divine ability that you have in your life is the anointing of the Holy Spirit.

I would now like to take a closer look at the purpose of the anointing as God's main criterion for ministry and at the role of revelation in manifesting the Spirit's power.

ANOINTING IS GOD'S FUNDAMENTAL CRITERION FOR MINISTRY

Every ministry or calling of God requires supernatural power and divine ability to execute it. This is the bar, or the minimum level, that God requires for a minister to be approved. God gives a purpose and an assignment to everything that He creates, but He also anoints it. Thus, each one of us as believers has been anointed according to the purpose and assignment that God has given us; we work for the Lord anointed for a specific assignment. When you find your purpose, you receive your anointing, and the supernatural power in your life intensifies.

> # The most frustrating thing in life is for a person to be anointed but not know why.

In the early days of their history, today's large denominations zealously upheld God's criterion of anointing and ensured that it was met. Nobody could teach or preach unless they had been baptized with the Holy Spirit and power. As we have seen, Jesus did not begin His public ministry until He was baptized in water and in the Holy Spirit. When His time had fully come, He went to the Jordan River hungry for more of God; as a Man, He was eager for an encounter with the Holy Spirit. He went to seek His anointing because He knew His purpose and wanted the power to fulfill it.

Jesus fulfilled the criterion! That is why the Scriptures refer to Him as *"Jesus of Nazareth, a Man attested by God to you by miracles, wonders, and signs which God did through Him in your midst"* (Acts 2:22).

Similarly, when Jesus was ready to entrust His disciples with the preaching of the gospel to the ends of the earth, He breathed on them the breath of the Holy Spirit (see John 20:22) before He ascended to sit at the right hand of the Father. He also gave them instructions not to leave Jerusalem until they had been endued with power from on high. (See Luke 24:49.)

> **God's criterion for ministry has always been and always will be an anointing with the Holy Spirit and power.**

To be approved by God, Jesus had to fulfill the same criterion of anointing as the prophets of old. Likewise, the anointing is required of any of us who want to minister to others in Jesus' name. But although, in the past, a person had to be approved, or certified, by God in order to exercise ministry, today's criteria for ministry in the church seems to be education, charisma, human talents, a good testimony, degrees from a Bible institute or seminary, a knowledge of denominational doctrine, and so forth.

Many instructors at Bible institutes and seminaries try to teach about God without having truly known or experienced Him. When a person preaches something they have never experienced, the only thing they can impart is mental knowledge or a purely rational biblical interpretation. In other words, no one can demonstrate God unless they have had an experience with Him, and that experience can only happen through an encounter with the Holy Spirit. Again, while I affirm that Bible study and biblical education are important, God's first criterion for ministry continues to be that a person have the anointing of the Holy Spirit, with the approval of the Father.

There are three things that Bible colleges and institutes cannot give: calling, anointing, and revelation. At our church, we have a Leadership Institute and a Bible university (University of the Supernatural Ministry) where we teach and train believers for ministry, but we ensure that the doctrine is confirmed by the Word and the Holy Spirit, and that we teach the progressive truth of God. It is not just about the letter of the Word. We put a great emphasis on students having experiences with God and on their being activated in supernatural power by the Holy Spirit.

As a whole, the church has been content with knowing *about* the Holy Spirit and the new birth but has been afraid to receive the baptism of the Holy Spirit and to walk in His power. But again, the confirmation that a ministry has been anointed by the Holy Spirit is the tangible and visible evidence of His supernatural power.

When John the Baptist was in jail, he sent several of his disciples to ask Jesus if He was the Messiah or if they should expect another. The answer that Jesus gave them was not based on arguments, Bible verses, or prophecies. He categorically replied using *evidences*, saying, without any doubt, "*Go and tell John the things which you hear and see: The blind see and the lame walk; the lepers are cleansed and the deaf hear; the dead are raised up and the poor have the gospel preached to them*" (Matthew 11:4–5).

John knew the Scriptures and understood that there was a guideline of anointing by which to recognize the Messiah who had been sent from God. Further, a common saying among the people at that time was, "When the Messiah comes, He will open the eyes of the blind and the ears of the deaf." (See Isaiah 35:5.) Thus, when the people saw that Jesus gave sight to the blind and hearing to the deaf, in affirmation of His teaching, they recognized that He was the Messiah. Even though Jesus was perfect and had no sin, He still needed to be approved by God with miracles, signs, and wonders such as healings. If you think that you do not need miracles, signs, and wonders in your ministry, then you think you are greater than Jesus.

Charisma, talent, and human ability have replaced the anointing.

We see many people in ministries working in their own strength and according to their own abilities. That is why they soon become discouraged and end up burning out. They continue to live according to tradition and know only a historical gospel, which is why they never experience the power of God. You don't have to be like that; as I wrote earlier, you are a candidate to be a carrier of the Holy Spirit and His power. If God was able to transform and use a religious person like the apostle Paul, He can use you and me. We all have the same potential to cast out demons and heal the sick, for we have been given the same Spirit and power. You are anointed to do "impossible" things!

The testimony of Apostle Jorge Ledesma from the city of Resistencia, in El Chaco, Argentina, perfectly illustrates the need to walk under the anointing of the Holy Spirit. The church he had founded several years previously, Iglesia Cristiana Internacional (International Christian Church), had been very closely connected with the most important revivals in the United States and South America. Each Sunday, eight thousand people would congregate at his church. However, he suddenly began to notice that there was a great spiritual void, and he could not understand the reason for it. About that time, the Holy Spirit spoke to his wife and told her, "They are not making room for Me at the church." The two of them then connected with our ministry, and this is what Apostle Jorge said happened next.

"My first encounter with King Jesus International Ministry was impactful. I discovered that we had abandoned the Holy Spirit, with whom we had moved years ago. I discovered the power of an apostolic church. But above all, I discovered fatherhood! All of that transformed our lives and ministry in a radical way.

"Once we submitted to Apostle Maldonado's spiritual covering, our services changed, and so did the church. We got into the river of the Spirit! After only five years of being with Apostle, our growth has multiplied. Today, over twenty-five thousand people fellowship with us each Sunday, and we continue to grow. We have built a new sanctuary with a capacity for eighteen thousand people—debt free. Further, we offer spiritual covering to other pastors and ministries who hunger and thirst for God, and they also are growing powerfully.

"Though our church had never faced financial troubles, when Apostle Maldonado visited us for the first time, our finances doubled in a matter of days, from the same number of people! It is important to stress that our church is located in one of the poorest provinces of Argentina, which makes the financial miracles and our great building a monument to the power of God.

"What demolished the old structures is a river of fresh revelation that we receive at every Supernatural Fivefold Ministry School (SFMS) and Apostolic and Prophetic Conference (CAP) at King Jesus Ministry. I had previously gotten used to receiving a great revelation and then working off of it for the following five or ten years. Now we understand that we must accelerate our steps to be in rhythm with God.

"Since we started to walk in the supernatural power of God, we have witnessed many miracles. These take place at each one of our six weekly services. In addition to thousands of other miracles, we have documented creative miracles. For example, people without an internal auditory canal suddenly heard clearly, women who'd had their uterus removed became pregnant, and vertebrae that had been destroyed were restored in minutes. I tend to summarize all of that with this declaration: 'The Holy Spirit is in His house, and He moves freely here!'"

> **If you preach and there are no supernatural signs that endorse your ministry, something is wrong.**

Today, many people go to church without having any expectation of seeing healings or miracles, because it is normal for nothing to happen at their services. Then, if they do see someone move in supernatural power, with miracles, signs, and wonders, they usually become suspect of that person, even deeming them a false prophet or false apostle. Everything is turned upside down! When I think of people going to church with no expectation that the Spirit will move, I ask myself, *Aren't you tired of sitting in churches that lack God's approval? How can you follow men who raise up ministries that don't have His endorsement?*

Those who attack the divine supernatural contradict Scripture and Christ Himself. Among them are people who greatly criticize the gospel of the kingdom. They criticize what they cannot produce themselves, and they invent doctrines to excuse their lack of power. But Jesus said, *"These signs will follow those who believe: in My name they will cast out demons; they will speak with new tongues…"* (Mark 16:17). If you have previously doubted or rejected the supernatural, I urge you to just believe what Jesus said so that He can give you revelation and so that, starting now, you can begin to have an anointed ministry approved by the Father.

The truth does not change; God will approve us the same way He approved Jesus. Only then will miracles, signs, and wonders follow us. In every country that I have visited, I have found many "Ichabod" churches and ministries. *Ichabod* means "no glory." (See 1 Samuel 4:21.) The glory of God has long since left them, and the presence of God is no longer there; but the worst thing is that they have not realized the glory has departed. They have the appearance of a Christian church, with doctrine and tradition, but they lack the power because the Holy Spirit is not present.

Do you have God's approval? Have you been supernaturally empowered with the Holy Spirit? Has God used you to give sight to the blind, to cause the lame to walk, or to raise the dead? Has God used you to cast out demons? If God has used you to work miracles, to deliver the oppressed, and to bring heaven to earth by the power of the Holy Spirit, then you are approved by the Father.

The anointing is the divine approval that affirms your calling and purpose in God.

Remember that you have been supernaturally empowered by God and anointed to do impossible things and to think above the *status quo*. You are anointed to deliver people from spiritual bondage placed on them by the enemy. You are anointed to bring transformation to people, places, and things; to change nations; to be productive and fruitful. You are anointed to confront and challenge the established order when it contradicts God and His way of approving and anointing His children for ministry.

Never say that you cannot do something, or that it is too difficult. You have divine abilities! You are anointed to manifest the power and the glory of God. Christ commissioned you when He said, *"And as you go, preach, saying, 'The kingdom of heaven is at hand.' Heal the sick, cleanse the lepers, raise the dead, cast out demons. Freely you have received, freely give"* (Matthew 10:7–8). From now on, as you go through life, whenever you see a sick person, tell yourself, *I have divine ability*, and minister to that person. For example, if you have been baptized with the Holy Spirit with the evidence of speaking in tongues and you see someone in a wheelchair, say, *I have been supernaturally empowered to heal the lame.* If you find someone who has just died, be filled with boldness from the Holy Spirit and say, *I have been supernaturally empowered to raise the dead.* Act in the same manner if you need to cast out demons, restore a marriage, rebuke the spirit of poverty, or bring the kingdom of heaven to earth in any other area. Do not be afraid to confront demons that are torturing people. Always act under the guidance of the Spirit of God, knowing that He who sent you will back you up in everything you endeavor, in the name of Jesus.

You do not have to be a pastor to cast out demons and raise the dead. You do not have to be perfect, either. If God were looking for someone who was perfect, He could never manifest His power. You only need to be available to be used by God, and to have a heart that is hungry to see people set free. God will then use you to manifest His supernatural power.

Power that is not used to fulfill the plans, will, and purpose of God is corrupted power.

REVELATION IS THE KEY TO DEMONSTRATION!

The key to all this is for us to receive revelation through the Holy Spirit and put it into practice, because the Spirit's purpose is to glorify, reveal, and manifest Jesus Christ—using us as His instruments. According to the Scriptures, the Holy Spirit's major assignment is to impart power to believers. That is why it says, *"You shall receive power when the Holy Spirit has come upon you; and you shall be witnesses to Me in Jerusalem, and in all Judea and Samaria, and to the end of the earth"* (Acts

1:8). The basis for manifesting the Spirit's power is to accept His revealed knowledge, which comes to us when we seek it. We must first accept the revelation that God wants us to demonstrate His supernatural power, and we must also seek the revelation of what the Spirit is saying to us in a particular situation, listening carefully to what He says. When the Holy Spirit comes upon us regularly, revelation becomes something normal to us rather than something foreign. Without revelation, we are ignorant of spiritual truths and run the risk of using the power of God incorrectly. Once you have an understanding of these things, you will realize that the Holy Spirit wants to move and manifest His power through you. And revealed knowledge is the key!

Whenever we have revealed knowledge, we are ready to manifest His power. Are you ready to fulfill the purpose of God? We are the demonstrators, the legal witnesses, of Jesus Christ, anointed to do the impossible in His name. Are you ready to say, "Yes, I want to demonstrate the power of God"? Are you prepared to step out of the boat and walk upon the water like Peter did?

To live in the anointing, you do not have to attend a Bible institute for years. At our church, there are believers who have been saved only a few weeks and are already casting out demons and healing the sick. That is because it is not a matter of talent but of the power of the Holy Spirit, and He is already in us. Will you make a decision today to demonstrate the power of God everywhere you go? This is the purpose and assignment of the Holy Spirit in your life.

Revealed knowledge is the basis for manifesting and demonstrating the power of God, and is the key to being divinely equipped.

ACTIVATION

If you want to demonstrate supernatural power and be a legal witness of Jesus, with a ministry that is approved by God, I invite you to pray to the Holy Spirit, saying:

Holy Spirit, I come before You and ask for understanding so I can know the person of Jesus Christ. I am a child of God and, as such, I claim the right to be guided and led by You. Cause me to see, perceive, and hear Your holy voice. I desire to know the truth about myself, my spiritual life, my marriage, and everything around me. Reveal to me Jesus' finished work on the cross and His defeat of Satan, so I can overcome the enemy and enforce Your victory on earth. Bring conviction to my life about any hidden sin. I don't want to offend You or quench You.

Precious Holy Spirit, there are so many things that I don't know, and I ask You to teach me. I cry out that Your anointing would come upon me now as I pray so that I can be a legal witness of Jesus Christ. May I understand that I am anointed to do miracles, signs, and wonders, to testify about Jesus, and to guide people to salvation through Christ. Anoint me with divine ability to do the impossible. Reveal Your word and Your knowledge to me so I can manifest Your power. Everywhere I go, I will manifest and demonstrate that Jesus is alive.

I don't want a religion or an appearance of godliness—I want the Holy Spirit. I want Your power, Your revelation, and Your truth. If there is any truth that I have rejected, I ask that You forgive me because I don't want to fall into deception. From now on, I will obey and walk as Jesus walked in the power of the Holy Spirit, so that the supernatural will become the norm for me. Today, I have an encounter with You, and I am anointed to do the impossible. In the name of Jesus, I receive it now! Amen!

REJECTING THE PERSON AND THINGS OF THE SPIRIT

For a very long time, philosophy has fought to overthrow biblical theology, but it continues to fail in its attempt. Philosophy is the love of human knowledge; it is the science that tries to answer the biggest questions that plague men, such as the origin of the universe, the meaning of life, and all matters relating to them as seen from a natural perspective. In contrast, biblical theology is the science that helps us see things from the perspective of heaven; it shows us how the Scriptures testify of the glory of God in the work of Jesus (see Luke 24:27) and in the person and power of the Holy Spirit, who inspired the entire Bible. In fact, the Bible affirms that when men and women of God spoke prophecy, they were always inspired by the Holy Spirit. (See 2 Peter 1:21.)

The conflict between philosophy and biblical theology occurs because philosophy attempts to study and understand God based on reason, which is impossible. Only the revelation that the Holy Spirit brings can reveal God to us in His infinite magnitude. Any branch of knowledge that lacks the supernatural component is void, empty, and even deceiving. In fact, even if we attend a Bible institute or earn a doctoral degree in theology, it does not guarantee that we will know the truth, because *"the natural man does not receive the things of the Spirit of God, for they are foolishness to him; nor can he know them, because they are spiritually discerned"* (1 Corinthians 2:14).

There are many who seek logical explanations alone for life's questions and end up completely separated from the truth. In the process, they relegate Jesus to the category of just one more philosopher. I know a number of people who hold several degrees, and because of their "higher learning," they have developed their own opinions about God apart from the truths of Scripture. Their knowledge has taken them away from the truth, and they live far from the revelation that the Spirit of God offers.

Many religions believe in the principles of God, but not in His supernatural power.

Nowadays, it is common to hear teachings about the Spirit of God and even "the things of the Spirit," but the idea of the supernatural is not popular; in fact, it is offensive to certain people. The supernatural involves miracles, signs, and wonders; the gifts of the Spirit; the revelation of the mysteries of God; God's will for every season of the church and the lives of individual believers; transformation of spirit, mind, and body; the casting out of demons; the raising of the dead, and more.

The Spirit operates in the eternal realm, a much higher level than simple reason. The carnal man operates only according to his five physical senses. Thus, he does not understand the things of heaven; he cannot discern the things that originate in the Spirit. His mind comprehends only what is logical from a human standpoint.

Western society, which is focused on self-sufficiency, individuality, and immediate satisfaction, has made education, reason, and logic its new gods. It has replaced all things spiritual for natural things, considering the supernatural power of God to be something that is unintellectual or obsolete. As a result, this generation respects only what can be scientifically tested, empirically measured, and logically analyzed. This frame of mind—which our contemporary culture has been reduced to—denies the power of God. It is natural that the knowledge of God would be suppressed in schools and universities where the spirit of the world operates and where knowledge is worshipped as the source of all things. For this very reason, the educational systems in many nations across the globe have removed God from their curriculums, so that He is now hidden and never discussed. Students are educated in a world that remains spiritually dark, and they are trained daily to deny the existence of God. However, more than one god cannot live in the same realm, so either our Lord Jesus Christ reigns, or another god does.

I must reemphasize here that I am not against the educational system, nor opposed to people studying and becoming knowledgeable. On the contrary, I always encourage the youth of our church to obtain higher education, to receive training, to gain knowledge, and to become prepared and equipped with the necessary skills for a secular job. However, this education and knowledge should not suppress or change their way of thinking about God based on the Bible and God's revealed word.

How can we prepare our children so they will not fall into deceit and lose their faith? The younger generation must always be educated while receiving the revealed knowledge that the Spirit of God brings, so they can live above and beyond natural knowledge. They also need to know what they face when they enter a university. That way they can discern the good from the bad, and keep that which will edify them. They have to be taught the right path, so that they may never be apart from the Lord. (See Proverbs 22:6.) If the church does not teach God's truth and revealed knowledge, our young people will believe everything that is taught to them in the philosophical theories imparted by the system of the world, and they will become an entire generation that goes against God.

> **Our children must know Jesus and His redeeming work on the cross, as well as the Holy Spirit, because He will lead them to all truth.**

Yet even sadder than this is the fact that we find the same problem in the church. Over the years, the spirit of antichrist has infiltrated the way we approach God. Nowadays, in churches, we see that everything goes well as long as the supernatural and the Holy Spirit are not mentioned. Otherwise, there is controversy. Yet every human being has a deep need for God that cannot be met by theological premises or philosophical analyses. The church is always in great need of the Holy Spirit and His supernatural power, especially in these times of darkness and mixture of beliefs.

Therefore, I don't believe the real problem comes from the atmosphere and mind-set that secular education creates, but from a lack of knowledge in the church about the world's rejection of the Holy Spirit. If we don't know about this paradigm, how can we fight against it? Additionally, when we do recognize it, we must understand that the Bible eternally establishes the principle that we win spiritual battles *"not by might nor by power, but by My Spirit,' says the LORD of hosts"* (Zechariah 4:6). We can apply this verse by saying, "Not by logic nor by philosophy, but by the Spirit of God." Although the natural realm is dominated by reason and scientific thought, the supernatural power of the Holy Spirit can invade the natural realm and break the laws of space, time, and matter.

> The more the church tries to please people, the less it will want to seek the Holy Spirit and His works.

THE SYSTEM OF THIS WORLD REJECTS THE SPIRIT OF GOD

Let us now analyze various ways in which both the world and the church reject the Holy Spirit, and then we will look at the resulting consequences.

1. A REJECTION OF THE PERSON OF THE HOLY SPIRIT

We have seen that rejecting the person of the Spirit of God is not just something unbelievers do, but something we see in the church as well. When His presence manifests in the middle of a service, many leaders ignore it and continue with their prepared schedules, without leaving room for Him to move among His people. These leaders do not care! They don't really want Him in the church! This is the reason why He remains grieved and quenched in so many congregations, remaining quiet for a long period of time, and rarely manifesting. Instead of seeking His guidance, the leaders have decided to conduct the church according to their own personal agendas, worshipping God "their way," rushing through the service, making "vain repetitions" (see Matthew 6:7), singing the same old songs, and preaching without revelation.

Their arrogant attitude shouts to the world that they think they know best what should transpire in church, considering themselves to be above the Holy Spirit. Consequently, they repress the manifestations of the gifts of the Spirit, including words of knowledge, prophecy, faith, healing, miracles, the discerning of spirits, and speaking in or interpreting tongues. This is the equivalent of a guest telling the owner of a house, "I am the one in charge here." It is the same as usurping authority.

The Holy Spirit goes where He is welcome, remains where He is recognized, and moves where He is given freedom.

We must be aware that the Holy Spirit only goes where He is celebrated, where He is treated as a Person sent by Christ—not where He is merely tolerated. The Scripture says that in Him, *"we all...are being transformed into the same image from glory to glory, just as by the Spirit of the Lord"* (2 Corinthians 3:18). The origin of all things in God is the Holy Spirit. If you do not want Him, you also will not want anything that comes from Him—you will not have a relationship with the Spirit of God, you will become disconnected from the life of Christ, and as a result, you will stop being transformed into His image. What is left will no longer be of God, but just a religion, a cultural practice or tradition. But when you desire the person of the Holy Spirit, when you know Him and give Him the place He deserves, then a passion for God and His power will be rekindled in you. You will become more sensitive to the spiritual world and start to recognize what does and does not come from God. A genuine zeal for that which comes from the Spirit will begin to grow within you.

Additionally, when we reject the person and things of the Spirit of God, we also reject Jesus as the Head of the church. The Son said He would send the Holy Spirit as the One who would reveal Him and His truth, who would be Administrator of the gifts, to carry forward Jesus's ministry on earth; the Spirit would be the very power by which we would exercise the anointing to do miracles, signs, and wonders in His name. Thus, we can see that if we reject the Holy Spirit, we also reject Christ's authority over His body, the church.

> **You cannot reject the things of God and say you believe in the Holy Spirit.**

2. A REJECTION OF THE SUPERNATURAL POWER OF THE HOLY SPIRIT

Out of the seven attributes of the Holy Spirit mentioned in Isaiah 11:2, the one that seems to be rejected the most is *"the Spirit…of might,"* or the spirit of power. At the time of the church's birth, all aspects of the Spirit flowed freely, and there was an emphasis on His power. I ask you, can the Holy Spirit be characterized without the element of power? Can He work without the ingredient of the supernatural? Can He be defined without including miracles or the casting out of demons? When the person, the things, and the supernatural power of the Holy Spirit are removed, there is no church left. Consequently, there is no more confrontation against Satan and the powers of hell.

It is as if modern Christianity believes that God has changed, that He is no longer almighty; that if miracles and supernatural manifestations once occurred, they are now a thing of the past with Jesus. As I mentioned previously, most Christians have no expectation that something supernatural will happen in their congregations, their homes, or their cities. They have reduced the Lord to the measure of man, thinking they can reject the role for which God created them and resist the purposes of the Creator.

However, God continues to be God. He has not changed, and He is still the Creator and Owner of the universe and everything in it. Jesus Christ continues to be the Redeemer of a fallen race. (See, for example, Hebrews 13:8.) Mankind could not sustain itself if God did not provide the breath of life; more important, we could not attain eternal life without the finished work of Jesus on the cross. God is our Father; He loves us as much as He loves Jesus, and He has provided the way for us to have an intimate relationship with Him. However, this does not mean we can forget that He is sovereign—that He is the Head and Supreme Authority over all creation. As created beings, we do not give orders to the Creator.

Earlier, we discussed how one of the functions of the Holy Spirit is to testify about Jesus and reveal Him to us. If this is the case, how can someone say they believe in Jesus while denying one of His most outstanding characteristics—His supernatural life? How can they not believe in His power if everything about Jesus is supernatural—His birth, ministry, resurrection, and more? How can someone reject the supernatural and still believe they can be filled with the Holy Spirit? In the same way, we cannot know the Holy Spirit while denying His power and miracles! It is like saying that you know, love, and accept someone but hate who they are.

You cannot say you know the Holy Spirit while, at the same time, denying the supernatural and being a stranger to His miracles.

Satan could not hold Jesus back from fulfilling the plan of salvation. However, although the enemy couldn't stop Jesus from finishing His work on the cross, he still tries to attack God's children. As we have seen, the next stage of his plan to defeat the Son of God is to go against the church. Because He could not stop the church from being born under the supernatural power of the Holy Spirit, his plan ever since has been to destroy God's people at all costs. To do that, he contaminates the spiritual atmosphere of the earth with false doctrines, in order to turn the church into something natural rather than spiritual, lacking the power of God. The enemy finds it easy to turn the church into a syncretism, or a system that mixes several doctrines, so that it compromises the truth and the principles of God.

> ## The master plan of the enemy is to make the church a natural entity, empty of the supernatural power of the Holy Spirit.

When a church falls into this trap, it stops being a threat to the enemy, since it no longer has the weapons to fight against him. As a result, it becomes irrelevant to its community. If it was once a light in the darkness, it has now become a refuge for religious traditionalists; if the church genuinely worshipped God before, it has now become an institution that merely flatters its members. If the church once allowed the Spirit of God to move among His people and bring conviction of sin, it has now been changed into a lifeless entity that excuses sin and pleases people instead of God. In such churches, God was once given first place, but now the leader has often become the star of the show and is essentially treated as if he is above God.

After traveling to nearly sixty countries, I can testify that most churches don't want the supernatural power of God. No one had to tell me this; I have seen it with my own eyes. For example, there is resistance toward speaking in tongues, because these churches don't want to offend people. Those who think this way prefer to please people first, even if doing so would displease God. Because of this, they lose the life of the Spirit, becoming dry and stagnant. In the same way, many leaders believe they can direct a ministry without the Holy Spirit and His supernatural power; they see ministry as a career or profession, not as a calling from God. However, this shouldn't surprise us because it is the same attitude that man has had toward His Creator since the beginning. Again, all we need to do is look at the first man and the first woman in Eden—disobeying God, rebelling against their Creator, and wanting to do things according to their own abilities.

A career is achieved by natural means, but a calling can only be carried out supernaturally.

REJECTING THE HOLY SPIRIT IS THE BEGINNING OF APOSTASY

For it is impossible for those who were once enlightened, and have tasted the heavenly gift, and have become partakers of the Holy Spirit, and have tasted the good word of God and the powers of the age to come, if they fall away, to renew them again to repentance, since they crucify again for themselves the Son of God, and put Him to an open shame. (Hebrews 6:4–6)

When people separate themselves from their faith in order to go after natural substitutes—when they start to live in a state of pseudo-spirituality—we can say they are facing the beginning of apostasy. Soon they are led by modern, temporal beliefs, and not by the eternal truths of Jesus, which are revealed by His Holy Spirit.

The word *apostasy* comes from the Latin *apostasia*, from the Greek *aphistasthai*. The Greek word is derived from *apo*, which means "outside of," and *histasthai*, "to stand." In the spiritual world, *apostasy* means to stand outside of the truth. It means to disassociate with, or renounce, the faith. Its synonyms are *abandonment, blasphemy, desertion, disloyalty, renouncement, retraction,* and *betrayal.* We live in times when the church is renouncing and dissociating itself from the person and things of the Spirit, as well as from the supernatural. This is not simply a trend or an innocent problem. It is Satan's plan. Again, the ultimate goal of the enemy is for the church to reject the supernatural, and to end up renouncing Jesus Christ. This is the spirit of antichrist and the beginning of apostasy.

In 1 John 2:18, we read, "*Little children, it is the last hour; and as you have heard that the Antichrist is coming, even now many antichrists have come, by which we know that it is the last hour.*" The prefix *anti-* in "*antichrists*" also comes from the Greek language and means "opposite" or "with contrary properties." The spirit of antichrist opposes Jesus and tries to replace what He represents. It hates everything that has to do with Jesus as the Anointed One, with the power of God, and with the cross. The anointing is the power of God that operates through us. Thus, when someone puts aside the supernatural and rejects the Holy Spirit, they have immediately placed a foot in the abyss, and they run the risk of the apostasy of their faith. What's worse, when they oppose Jesus Himself, they show they have given room in their lives to the spirit of antichrist.

A pastor in my city used to laugh at me and mock the manifestations of the Holy Spirit in my church. He would frequently attack me for these things, and one day he even started to openly oppose the movement of the Spirit. A short time later, he was arrested for breaking the law and ended up in jail. This led him to lose his ministry and everything he had. What I want to show by this illustration is that you cannot fight against the Holy Spirit, because sooner or later the judgment of God will come upon you. When the spirit of antichrist influences a person's life, they start to speak poorly of the Spirit, of His works, and of the supernatural; this leads them to then compromise the principles of God and to divorce themselves from His Spirit, and ultimately to renounce their faith in Jesus.

> **The beginning of apostasy is the rejection of the Holy Spirit, the things of the Spirit, and His supernatural power.**

CONSEQUENCES OF REJECTING THE HOLY SPIRIT

When the person, things, and power of the Holy Spirit are removed from a church or the life of a believer, it will have the following consequences. Some of these consequences overlap, but each one is vital to consider separately.

WE CANNOT BE BORN AGAIN

First, we cannot even be born again without the Spirit.

Nicodemus said to [Jesus], "How can a man be born when he is old? Can he enter a second time into his mother's womb and be born?" Jesus answered, "Most assuredly, I say to you, unless one is born of water and the Spirit, he cannot enter the kingdom of God."

(John 3:4–5)

Being "born again" is not a religious experience. It is a divine work that is started and finished in the Holy Spirit, and is directly related to continued spiritual growth. Being born again means to start a new life, from zero. When we accept the plan of God for salvation, we are transferred in the Spirit from death to life. We receive the life of Christ! God gives us His nature, and the Holy Spirit comes to dwell in us. That is why, if we reject the Spirit, our lives cannot be transformed.

WE CANNOT KNOW JESUS

Jesus made it very clear that we would need the Holy Spirit in order to know Him. He stated this reality to His disciples when He said, *"When the Helper comes, whom I shall send to you from the Father, the Spirit of truth who proceeds from the Father, He will testify of Me"* (John 15:26). The Holy Spirit is the One who reveals Jesus to us; we cannot know the Son without Him. We saw that when Jesus was baptized in the Jordan, the Spirit came upon Him in the form of a dove, testifying that He was the Son of God. And 1 John 5:6 says, *"It is the Spirit who bears witness, because the Spirit is truth."* This verse is in present tense, meaning that although this happened over two thousand years ago, the Spirit continues to testify about Jesus and reveal Him to us, now and for all eternity.

THE PRESENCE OF GOD LIFTS FROM US

In the Old Testament, the Spirit was removed from the Israelites, and the people called it *Ichabod*, which again in Hebrew means "without glory," or "the glory has left Israel." (See 1 Samuel 4:21.) At that time, the glory or presence of God was lifted from Israel because of the abundance of its rebellion, sin, and idolatry.

When we remove the Holy Spirit from our lives, the presence of God leaves us. Jesus was very aware of this spiritual possibility, and He never wanted the presence of the Father to abandon Him. However, in order for His purpose upon the earth to be fulfilled, this is exactly what had to happen. Nailed to the cross and carrying upon Himself the sins of all humanity across all times, He desperately cried out, *"My God, My God, why have You forsaken Me?*" (Matthew 27:46). Today, we live in times when every believer should have that same holy fear, so that the presence of God may never be absent from us or gone from our lives. Cry out to the Father and say, "Lord, do not cast me out from Your presence, and do not remove Your Holy Spirit from me." (See Psalm 51:11.)

THE BIBLE BECOMES ONLY THE LETTER OF THE LAW, WITHOUT LIFE

"[God]...*also made us sufficient as ministers of the new covenant, not of the letter but of the Spirit; for the letter kills, but the Spirit gives life*" (2 Corinthians 3:6). As children of God, born of the Spirit, we are "ministers of a new covenant," one that is based on God's promise, which is alive and effective, and which is revealed through the Scriptures.

However, we must be careful not to place the Bible above the Holy Spirit, for He is the One who inspired God's Word, who opens the Scriptures to us and gives life to them. Though both the Word and the Spirit are important, the Bible needs to be revealed to us by the Holy Spirit so that it can impact and transform our lives. The central idea is that we cannot simply know the words of the Bible in order to appear wise; rather, we must follow the Holy Spirit through the Scriptures.

WE BECOME STAGNANT IN ALL AREAS

If there are areas in our lives that never change, we are in a stagnant state. Stagnancy does not come from God or live in His divine nature. If we are indeed children of God, born again and filled with the Holy Spirit, then stagnancy cannot be part of our lives—it is unnatural for those who belong to God's family! The nature of heaven implies growth, advancement, and conquest. That is our spiritual DNA!

The Holy Spirit is the One who changes and transforms us; He is the One who makes us grow "*to the measure of the stature of the fullness of Christ*" (Ephesians 4:13). If the Spirit is not inside us, we will not receive His revelation for each area in which we need to change.

Even worse than this, the Holy Spirit will not lead us to Jesus to be delivered, or change our heart so we can be separated from sin. The presence of the Holy Spirit in our lives is what leads to a constant life of growth.

WE ARE LEFT WITH A "FORM OF GODLINESS," MERE RELIGION, AND INSTITUTIONS

When we reject the Holy Spirit, and He lifts His presence from us, all we are left with is a religion, or simply a "Christian" way of living. We go to church, sing the right songs, speak in a Christian vocabulary, and listen to sermons. Yet absolutely nothing in our life is changed. We arrive sick and leave sick; we go depressed and return home the same way; we bring the problems in our marriage, and we leave with them. There is no transformation. For this reason, many people become discouraged or disillusioned about their faith, and they go back to their old coping mechanisms to deal with their problems, such as taking illegal drugs, drinking to excess, and smoking cigarettes; they keep the old depression, lies, adultery, and other sins.

When this is the case, we are dealing with something that looks like a church but does not act like one, because it does not change the lives of its members or meet the needs of the lost world around it. It has become a collection of old practices—an institution of mere religious "repetition." What once was founded to present Jesus to the world has become nothing more than a human organization, a social club, or even a charity. None of these things is bad in itself, but it is far from the purpose for which the true church of Christ was created.

What should we do when we encounter people *"having a form of godliness but denying its power"* (2 Timothy 3:5)—who do not want to repent, who insist on rejecting the work of the Holy Spirit and His power? The Bible warns us that every time we face these kinds of people, we must separate from them; the apostle Paul concludes, *"From such people turn away"* (verse 5).

The appearance of godliness is merely an external form of something that does not exist in reality on the inside; it lacks the power of God.

WE CANNOT DRAW CLOSER TO GOD

The Holy Spirit reveals the truth; He is the One who opens our spiritual eyes to see the Lord and equips us with spiritual gifts that work in the eternal realm. The Spirit came to reveal the Father to us and to give us the grace and faith to believe in the redeeming work of Jesus on the cross of Calvary. Without the Holy Spirit we cannot draw closer to the Lord; therefore, if we reject the Holy Spirit, we reject God, and He will stop manifesting Himself in our lives. The three members of the Godhead are One and cannot be separated. You cannot receive One and hate the Other, because then you reject all Three. *"He who receives whomever I send receives Me; and he who receives Me receives Him who sent Me"* (John 13:20).

THE JUDGMENT OF GOD COMES

The judgment of God falls on those who know the truth yet still choose substitutes for it. *"For the time has come for judgment to begin at the house of God"* (1 Peter 4:17). I believe God will judge those who grieve, quench, and reject the Spirit and His works just so they can please man.

I have seen the judgment of God! In addition to the pastor I described earlier, I know other pastors who have prohibited their congregations from speaking in tongues, believing in miracles, and casting out demons, and who have even dared to give credit to the enemy for things the Holy Spirit has done. I have seen pastors die without fulfilling their purpose on earth; I have seen congregations go from being megachurches to closing their doors in just a few months. For this reason, I have a burning desire in my heart to fight for the things of the Spirit and to have the church return to the Holy Spirit and the power of God. I believe this is the will of God, and I want to fulfill it. It hurts me to see so many leaders and believers go back to the desires of the flesh and to their old way of doing things, and lose their hunger for God, because they are deceived with regard to the Spirit.

Many people who attend King Jesus Ministry today once went to other churches, some of whose pastors did not believe in speaking in tongues or the movement of the Holy Spirit. In one instance, several of these people went back to visit their previous congregation, and when the pastor heard them pray, he told them to be quiet. He did not believe that the Holy Spirit would move in his church; neither did he want it to happen. Years later, that pastor was kicked out by the church's board.

First Timothy 4:1–2 affirms, "*The Spirit expressly says that in latter times some will depart from the faith, giving heed to deceiving spirits and doctrines of demons, speaking lies in hypocrisy, having their own conscience seared with a hot iron*"—doing what displeases the Lord. As we can see, in the end times there will be an increase of doctrines that aim to please people rather than honor and serve God. But the Holy Spirit is not among us to please people; He is not here for those who are merely looking for a church that suits their own beliefs and philosophies. He is here to carry out the will of God.

THE CHURCH BECOMES AN ILLEGAL WITNESS, LACKING THE HOLY SPIRIT AND HIS POWER

Jesus set the standard for living by the Spirit when He went to the Jordan to be empowered by the baptism of the Holy Spirit. In that moment, He became a legal witness of the Father and was filled with the power of God. As we have seen, He did not begin His ministry or do miracles without first being sent out and empowered by the Agent of the anointing, which is the Holy Spirit. Even He didn't dare to teach or preach without the backing of the supernatural. Although He was God,

Jesus did not use His title to show off, but instead followed the principles of the kingdom in order to legally exercise His ministry on the earth.

> **The true house of God defines itself by the power it holds. Without the power of the Holy Spirit, the believer will be an illegal witness.**

Sometimes, church leaders send people to work in the ministry armed with knowledge but completely lacking the power of the Holy Spirit. In contrast, Jesus sent out His disciples upon a foundation of power, the same foundation that He had. Oftentimes, we don't follow this example but instead violate the principles of the kingdom by doing things according to our own logic, strength, and beliefs, without relying on the supernatural power of God. Only the active presence of the Holy Spirit gives us the legal right to minister in His name.

THE CHURCH STOPS BEING A HOUSE OF GOD AND BECOMES A HOUSE OF MAN

The Bible often depicts the setting apart of two opposing houses— one earthly, one spiritual. For example, the house of Saul and the house of David, or the house of Esau and the house of Jacob. In the second case, Jacob represented Israel, which is the house of God, while Esau represented the house of man. In the house of man, there is human activity but no spiritual activity; there are no miracles, signs, or wonders; there is no deliverance or supernatural power; there is no transformation or change in the heart. There is no life of God! There are ministries that have great attendance and a lot of activity, but God is not pleased with them because they are spiritually immature and have become merely social gatherings.

In the house of God, there is life and a strong movement of the Spirit, with miracles, healings, restored marriages, and heart transformations; individuals are changed, demons are cast out, and the dead are raised. There is legitimate spiritual activity in the house of the Lord because He dwells there. The question is, what house do you want to live in? Do you want to be in the house of man or the house of God?

THE CHURCH BECOMES MERELY A NATURAL ENTITY

When the church compromises the truth and principles of God, it loses its ability to manifest His supernatural power and to supply the needs of people. Rejecting the Holy Spirit and His works leaves the church powerless to fight against sin, sickness, misery, poverty, death, and all the works of the enemy. This causes the church to become a natural entity, a human institution. You cannot defeat that which you tolerate; this is why the Word says, *"Do not be overcome by evil, but overcome evil with good"* (Romans 12:21).

THE CHURCH BECOMES INEFFECTIVE

Here, the key word is *ineffective*, because an ineffective church will soon become irrelevant. To be effective means to have the ability to achieve a desired outcome. A church's ability to be effective depends completely upon its relationship with the Spirit of truth and power. When it rejects the Holy Spirit, the church loses its relevance—its ability to make a genuine difference in society. If we want to have an eternal and permanent impact upon this generation, we cannot stray from the counsel and power of the Spirit of God.

Pastor Félix Orquera, of Iquique, Chile, has one of the largest and most prosperous churches in his country because he chose to accept the guidance of the Holy Spirit. Yet things weren't like this only ten years ago. At that time, he had just under seventy people in his congregation, and his finances were suffering. But he had a dream to impact his generation, and what he heard from God touched his life forever. This is his testimony.

"It was the second time I saw Apostle Maldonado's show on Enlace TV—the Spanish station of the Trinity Broadcasting Network (TBN)—when I heard God tell me, 'I have given you the servant you see before you as a spiritual father,' and this really shook up my life!

"I immediately called King Jesus Ministry, seeking to be under their covering, but I was told I would have to travel to Miami. Once there, we were received warmly and taught about the vision God had given to the Apostle. Once I spoke with him, I was surprised by his words. He said, 'Son, if you say that God spoke to you, I believe you, but let me pray too; when He confirms it to me, I will give you my fatherhood.' This gave me such a strong sense of security that I knew I was in the right place. He then opened the doors of his ministry to me and said, 'Everything you see here, you can use and implement for your people.'

"By the time my wife and I went back to Chile, we were no longer the same. That trip changed us! Miracles began to manifest in our church, and the Holy Spirit started moving in our favor. The church soon grew to two hundred members, but our desire was to win the whole city for Jesus. Today, we have a local church of eighteen hundred members, two daughter churches, and thirty-eight churches under our covering across Chile, Argentina, Bolivia, Brazil, and Peru.

"Our church moves in the supernatural power of God, and we frequently witness financial miracles, but the most impactful part is that ever since we went under the spiritual covering of Apostle Maldonado, the healings and creative miracles that the Lord has done in our church have been too many to count! One day, we were asked to pray for a girl who was very seriously ill in the hospital. The next day she died, but we continued to declare life and healing over her because we didn't know she had died. The family shares that when they were at the morgue, discussing the details for the girl's funeral, they heard cries of, 'Mama! Mama!' When they ran to see who was calling, they found their daughter, who had been dead for two hours, returned to life and completely healthy!

The Holy Spirit Himself touched her, and breathed new life over her! To God be the glory!"

This is an example of a truly effective church that is making a difference in the place of its assignment!

THE CHURCH BECOMES JUST AN ENTERTAINMENT CENTER

In a church where the Spirit of God is suppressed and does not move, the praise and worship become nothing more than a concert. Likewise, the sermons are simply motivational messages that lack the power to lead people to grow in their faith and mature, and to manifest the supernatural in their lives.

When you have the Holy Spirit and His power, there is no room for worldly points of view to come into your life and distort the truth. If you love God and want to see His glory manifested, you will not want your church to be merely an entertainment center. You will pay the price of rejection and opposition in order to have the presence and the truth of the Holy Spirit in your congregation. You will wait for the fulfillment of the promise that says, *"Blessed are you when they revile and persecute you, and say all kinds of evil against you falsely for My sake. Rejoice and be exceedingly glad, for great is your reward in heaven"* (Matthew 5:11–12).

> **Without the Holy Spirit and His power, Christianity is simply entertainment.**

THE CHURCH CANNOT OVERCOME THE IMPOSSIBLE CIRCUMSTANCES OF MANKIND

We live in times of dramatic change; advancements in technology, science, and communications have forever altered society's panorama.

However, though science proposes many solutions, we continue to face situations that are impossible to resolve. Serious illness, death, hunger, poverty, loneliness, natural disasters, terrorism, financial crises, and additional hazards are challenges for a society that rejects God.

For example, for every cure that modern medicine derives for a disease, a new sickness is discovered. Every day, more pharmaceuticals are developed and more psychiatric treatments emerge, but people continue to die of illness, loneliness, depression, and other emotional problems. Meanwhile, nature is being altered by climate change, and we suffer from floods, forest fires, droughts, earthquakes, hurricanes, and tsunamis, leaving cities and nations devastated in their wake. The church does not often have answers for these impossible circumstances that befall mankind because it has lost the power of the Holy Spirit. There is no way to overcome adversity without the supernatural power of the Spirit of God.

But what happens when we welcome the Holy Spirit? God manifests His presence and moves with power! This is what happened during the last night of the Supernatural Encounter I held in West Palm Beach, Florida, an hour and a half north of Miami. The Holy Spirit told me that He wanted to bring creative miracles, so I called up all the people who needed a new organ or were missing a body part. That night, thirty-three creative miracles were recorded. The Lord made new bones, teeth, ovaries, thyroids, eardrums, and more. But the testimony of Jenyne Walker Nichols, a forty-year-old African-American woman, was the one that impacted me the most. This is what she shared.

"A year ago, I started suffering from a constant cough that wouldn't go away. When I went to the doctor, I was told I had signs of pneumonia, and I was prescribed antibiotics. For the next three months, my body rejected the medication, and the cough still wouldn't stop. On top of this, I started having high blood pressure and difficulties breathing, and I was constantly fatigued. I went to the hospital, and the doctor performed an X-ray of my lungs. He discovered that a heavy fluid was building up and making its way to my heart. I had to go through open heart surgery, and the doctors removed nearly seventy-five pounds of liquid! Unfortunately, they also discovered that my kidneys were failing because of the extended treatment of antibiotics.

"When my mother found out that Apostle Maldonado was coming to West Palm Beach, she invited me to the Supernatural Encounter. I attended in a wheelchair. I had always believed in God and knew He did miracles, but I also knew that many healings were progressive. However, when the Apostle declared that God was creating new kidneys, I got up from my wheelchair and dared to believe that word. As soon as he started to pray, the Holy Spirit came over me and hugged me, and I felt a strong heat on my back and in my womb. In that moment, I knew I had been healed, and I felt my strength being restored. My hands had turned dark due to the kidney failure, but when God touched me they went back to their original color, and I could not stop crying with joy! That night, I had the strong conviction that the Lord had created new kidneys in me, and days later I went to the doctor, where test results showed I was completely healed! What can I say? All I can do is shout to the world that God loves me!"

RETURNING TO COMMUNION WITH THE HOLY SPIRIT AND THE SUPERNATURAL

After reading and understanding the consequences that come from rejecting the Holy Spirit, and evaluating our lives in light of them, we cannot keep living the same way. We must renew our communion with the Spirit of Truth.

Throughout this chapter, we have seen the importance of the Holy Spirit's presence in our lives, our faith, and our churches. It is clear that although we may say we have faith in Christ, if we reject the Holy Spirit, thus following the spirit of antichrist, we risk falling into apostasy. Every time we find ourselves influenced by the spirit of deceit, which oppresses us and steals the life of God from us, we need to be delivered. Jesus Himself taught us, *"And you shall know the truth, and the truth shall make you free"* (John 8:32).

The truth is the highest level of reality, and it is present only where the Spirit of God dwells.

What is the truth? The truth is Jesus, who is represented on earth by the person of the Holy Spirit. The Bible says, *"However, when He, the Spirit of truth, has come, He will guide you into all truth; for He will not speak on His own authority, but whatever He hears He will speak; and He will tell you things to come"* (John 16:13). The Word also affirms, *"The Lord is the Spirit; and where the Spirit of the Lord is, there is liberty"* (2 Corinthians 3:17).

When we don't have the Holy Spirit, we don't have the truth, and we cannot discern between truth and falsehood. Someone who has had an experience with the Holy Spirit loves the truth and is hungry for it, because it is what delivers us from oppression.

Truth is also the basis of supernatural power, and this is the aspect of the work of the Holy Spirit that I have been emphasizing in this chapter. We have seen that, many times, when the truth manifests itself in a church, people reject it and say that it does not come from God. This happens when they are merely practicing an appearance of godliness and not living in His truth. It happened to the Pharisees, the Sadducees, and the scribes of Jesus' time. They lived an appearance of righteousness but could not recognize the Truth that was presented before them in flesh and blood. So remember, when you go forth to carry the truth and demonstrate the power of God, many people who hunger and thirst for Him will receive you, but many will reject you, as well, because not everyone likes the truth.

The problem many people have with the truth is that it exposes the false spiritual reality they are living in. It makes them face their problems and shows them their need to repent and change. This is something many people run away from because they are comfortable in their religion. Generally, neither the Pharisees nor the Sadducees received Jesus, because when He went to the synagogues, He exposed the reality they lived in, and they were not willing to humble themselves and change. Again, when the Holy Spirit is absent, the truth is not present; there is only a form, a tradition, or a false Christianity that lacks the power to change people's hearts.

> **There is no freedom without truth, and there is no truth without the Spirit of God.**

LET THE HOLY SPIRIT FLOW

We, the children of God, have rejected the Holy Spirit, the things of the Spirit, and His supernatural power. This has led us to lose the presence of God in our churches. As a result, we have lacked truth, spiritual growth, and the presence of our beloved Lord. We have become irrelevant and ineffective. We need to come back to the Holy Spirit so that He may reveal the truth to us, take us out of stagnancy, draw us closer to God, and stir up our inner being. We must permit the Holy Spirit to flow in our lives, surrender to Him, and allow Him to do His works, according to the will of the Father.

When I preach, I allow the Spirit to come over me with His power and take control. Before every service, I prepare myself in prayer, fasting, and studying the Word. This enables me to always have a message for God's people; but many times, the Lord has led me to preach a different message once I am in the pulpit. Other times, the Holy Spirit simply begins to move in miracles, healings, and deliverances. This is why I go to our services ready and willing to let Him move as He desires. I have a great fear of God and do not want to quench His power, because I know He always wants to do something supernatural among His people. That is why the life of the Spirit flows in our church, our homes, and our personal lives.

If you have been rejecting the Holy Spirit in relation to any of the things I have mentioned in this chapter; if you feel dry and empty inside; if the Holy Spirit does not flow inside you; if all you have is the appearance of God but not His power...what you are following is a human formula for life that has nothing to do with heaven. Repent!

If you are a minister in your church and recognize that the power and life of God are not present in your congregation, this is your opportunity to repent and cry out to Him, so that the Lord will make a vessel out of you that the Holy Spirit can use to heal and deliver others who are hungry for His transforming power.

As children of God, we owe the world an experience with the supernatural and the Holy Spirit.

Jesus told us that apart from Him, we can do nothing. If we are honest with ourselves, we will understand that we are powerless to answer people's needs if we don't have the Holy Spirit. We need to humble ourselves and recognize we cannot do the work of the ministry, supply people's needs, overcome the devil, and expand the kingdom of God without the person, the works, and the supernatural power of the Spirit.

Additionally, if you are going through a seemingly impossible situation—a sickness, a broken heart, a financial problem, a crisis in your marriage or family—this is the moment to cry out to the Spirit of God. You will never see how real the supernatural is until you have lived through an impossibility that only God can solve. Right now, He is telling you that He is ready to supply all of your needs. All you need to do is believe that He will do it!

ACTIVATION

Allow me to lead you to an intimate relationship with the person of the Holy Spirit. One day, David prayed desperately to God, *"Do not cast me away from Your presence, and do not take Your Holy Spirit from me"* (Psalm 51:11). Today, I want us to pray in that same manner. Join me as we ask God the Father to show us the areas where we have quenched His Holy Spirit, and in what ways we have offended His heart. Let *"the grace of the Lord Jesus Christ, and the love of God, and the communion of the Holy Spirit be with you all. Amen"* (2 Corinthians 13:14).

1. Prayer of repentance for having rejected the Holy Spirit:

Heavenly Father, in the name of Jesus, I repent for having rejected the person of the Holy Spirit in my life, my family, my church, my ministry, and my job or business. Today, I open my heart to the Holy Spirit so that He will come to my house, lead me, and empower me to live a holy and righteous life. I repent for having dissociated myself from the Holy Spirit, for rejecting, blaspheming, or speaking against the miracles, signs, and wonders, the supernatural, and the people who move in the Holy Spirit and speak in tongues. I repent in the name of Jesus. I ask You to forgive me and cleanse me by the Holy Spirit, and may the blood of Jesus wash away my sins, now!

2. Prayer for a miracle from God for an impossible situation:

This is the time to seek God about any impossibility you have. If you are sick, if you need deliverance, if you need the love of God, if you have a circumstance that needs changing, it's time to cry out! You can use the following sample prayer, but do so with a sincere heart:

> Father God, I cry out to You and ask You to show me the areas of my life where I need a miracle. These situations are impossible for me, and I need divine intervention. I remove every obstacle and call on Your supernatural grace now to overcome everything that is causing stagnation in my life. I ask at this moment that Your power may move in favor over my life. In the name of Jesus, amen.

5

THE DEMONSTRATION OF THE SPIRIT AND POWER

As the church, we are not carrying out the ministry of Jesus the way He lived it and taught it; thus, we are not truly following Him as His disciples. We are meant to do greater works than He (see John 14:12) and to walk by the grace of the Helper, but we have lost sight of the mandate and the promises Jesus gave us to continue His work on earth. We have stopped listening to His voice and obeying His mandate, and instead have tried to conform to a worldly society. Because the body of Christ has not understood the magnitude of the work that God has entrusted it with, it folds in on itself and bends to the circumstances around it.

The prophet Isaiah said, *"Therefore my people have gone into captivity, because they have no knowledge; their honorable men are famished, and their multitude dried up with thirst"* (Isaiah 5:13). Another prophet spoke on the same topic when he said that the people of God perish for their lack of knowledge. (See Hosea 4:6.) Because of an absence of revelation, the church teaches about the God of history instead of the God of the now. But the Lord's desire is for us to receive His knowledge, to live in it correctly, and to manifest His love and power for mankind today. (See Hosea 6:6.) Everything begins by living and experiencing what the Lord reveals to us, so that we can understand it, teach it, and demonstrate it.

The supernatural must be experienced in order to be understood.

UNDERSTANDING THE REVELATION AND POWER OF GOD

The following points will help us understand and demonstrate the revelation and power of God through the Spirit.

1. THE DIFFERENCE BETWEEN *LOGOS* AND *RHEMA*

First, I would like to establish the difference between these two important words in relation to receiving revelation from God: *logos* and *rhema*. Both terms refer to the Word of God, but they do so in different ways. If we practice only one aspect, our knowledge of the Lord will be unbalanced. As we proceed, remember that the *rhema* word is always in agreement with the *logos* word. One never contradicts the other.

The *logos* is the written Word of God, which, from Genesis to Revelation, was inspired by the Holy Spirit. (See 2 Timothy 3:16.) Jesus Himself is the Word that has existed from eternity, since before creation. He is the Word that exists in relation to God, the Word made flesh that dwells inside of us and leads us to the glory of God. (See John 1:1, 14.)

A *rhema* is a spoken word of God for today, for a specific situation. When the Bible tells us to take up *"the sword of the Spirit, which is the word of God"* (Ephesians 6:17), what it is asking is that we make a declaration of faith, that we decree an order according to His Word, full of the power of the Holy Spirit. As Christians, we must learn to use the *rhema* word as a sword in which to fight the attacks of the enemy, just as Jesus used it to fight against the attacks of the enemy when He was tempted in the desert by the devil. (See Matthew 4:1–11.)

> *Logos* is where our faith is established, but *rhema* is where our faith is activated.

One of the enemy's tricks is to keep Christians focused on the *logos* without the revelation. That is why many of us don't take steps of faith or demonstrate what we preach. Many of us believe but are not activated to live out what we believe. We have no problem with the written Word; it is the *rhema* about which we are divided. But to have the full knowledge of God and His will for us, we need the *rhema* word, which is the *logos* revealed in the now.

Logos, the written Word of God, is:

+ The basis of our faith.
+ The foundation of our doctrine.
+ The core of our belief system.

Rhema, the spoken and specific word of God, is:

+ The approval from heaven to move in the supernatural.

> **If someone wants to walk in the supernatural power of God, they undoubtedly need the *rhema* word.**

We know that Jesus had problems with the Pharisees and Sadducees, the religious leaders of the time. Members of both groups had strong educations, having studied the written Word—the Torah—for years, but they lacked revelation. Their knowledge sparked their pride, because they knew the doctrine, the Law, the commandments, the Prophets, and the Writings so well. They believed in the written Word, but not in the *rhema*. In other words, they had the letter of the Bible, but not its spirit. If they had, they would have received revelation and recognized who Jesus was.

2. THE DIFFERENCE BETWEEN THE WORD AND THE SPIRIT

The Bible is the Word of God, but the Spirit is the One who reveals it and manifests it with His power. The Scriptures establish the doctrine and the fundamental beliefs of Christianity, but the Spirit is the One who makes known that Word to us. That is why I believe the book of Acts was not written to show off the great works of the apostles but to highlight the work of the Holy Spirit, who transforms common people into true heroes of the faith.

To better understand this point, let's look at another example concerning the Sadducees. On a certain occasion, Jesus was interrogated by members of this group about the resurrection. Remember that these priests of the temple were very fond of religion, and they were constantly challenging Jesus with their knowledge of the Scriptures and trying to make Him fall into a trap to discredit Him. However, Jesus wisely answered, *"Your mistake is that you don't know the Scriptures, and you don't know the power of God"* (Mark 12:24 NLT).

> ## It is dangerous for a Christian to be full of the letter of the Scriptures but empty of the revealed Word, because the letter can destroy any revival of the Spirit.

The intellectual knowledge of the Sadducees was not enough for them to understand the Word. Because of their lack of revelation, the Sadducees saw God as a god of the dead; however, it was clear to Jesus that the Lord is the God of the living, and has the power to raise those who have died. Thus, a knowledge of the Scriptures alone is insufficient. It must be tied to the revealed knowledge of the power of God. Only those who both know the Word and have revelation from the Holy Spirit will walk in God's power.

The covers on Bibles should have a warning that says, "The letter without the Spirit kills." As Paul wrote, *"[God] made us sufficient as ministers of the new covenant, not of the letter but of the Spirit; for the letter kills, but the Spirit gives life"* (2 Corinthians 3:6). We need to depend on the Holy Spirit in order to understand the Word—so it can be revealed and take life in our spirit. Otherwise, it becomes impossible for us to live a Christian life, to walk in the truth, and to demonstrate the Word with power.

To demonstrate the power of God, we need revelation of the Word in the now.

In some families, the children prefer to be with their father, while in others, they want to be with their mother; what they don't see is the fact that they need both. There is a similar trend in the body of Christ. Some believers tend to go solely to the Word, based on verses like Luke 21:33, *"Heaven and earth will pass away, but My words will by no means pass away."* For other believers, everything is Spirit, and the Word is taken for granted. What is really biblical is to have a balance between them both. The two complement each other, and choosing one over the other can lead us down the wrong path. But these are times when God is lifting up a generation of both Word and Spirit.

3. THE DIFFERENCE BETWEEN THEORY AND PRACTICE

Theory has to do with the mental elaboration of an idea, a principle, or a belief; it is intangible. Practice, however, has to do with putting theory into practical action. The gospel that Jesus Christ came to preach is a permanent combination of both aspects, the theoretical and the practical. If gospel theory is separated from gospel practice, it automatically ceases to be the true gospel of the kingdom.

There are churches that carry the gospel well when it comes to calling people to repentance for sin and looking to Jesus for the salvation of their souls. But when it comes to the realm of finances, for example, they quickly separate theory from practice; their members do not tithe, only occasionally give offerings, do not sow financially into the lives of other people, and so on. It seems that if something is intangible, it is okay with them because it does not put any requirement on their external behavior or get people out of their comfort zone. However, when they are asked to live according to the gospel they preach, things become complicated, because their practice denies their theory.

The Bible is complete, but not everything has been revealed to us by the Spirit.

No knowledge is really yours until you practice it and live it. If what you believe remains a theory, it is nothing more than information. Under these circumstances, when you face adversity, disease, or crisis, gospel theory will not help you. Instead, you'll be as helpless as anyone who does not have God.

The gospel of the kingdom is not theory but power! (See 1 Corinthians 4:20.) This means that life is not about how much theory we know, but how much of that theory we put into effect.

How much of what you know do you actually practice? How much have you obeyed? How much of your knowledge have you experienced? One of the reasons why the church does not demonstrate the power of God is that the truths of the kingdom remain only in the minds of believers; we have not applied the power and revelation of the Word.

4. THE DIFFERENCE BETWEEN REVELATION AND MANIFESTATION

GENERAL REVELATION AND SPECIAL REVELATION

For our purposes, we can say that there are two types of revelation: (1) general revelation, which includes everything God has communicated about Himself, to every person, at all times, everywhere, and (2) special revelation, which is made up of God's communications to certain individuals, at specific times.

The spiritual reality you experience in the invisible realm must manifest itself in the physical realm and impact the natural world.

Revelation discloses a portion of the mind of God in the now. Manifestation is the tangible and visible proof of that revelation. Revelation and manifestation are interdependent, meaning that there is no revelation without spiritual manifestation, and vice versa. To operate on the earth as Jesus did, we must have both.

In saying that revelation is the requirement for demonstrating the power of God, I restate the fact that mere information and fallen knowledge do not transform people. The things that fail to produce revelation do not allow change in the individual because the power of the Holy Spirit does not manifest inside the person. However, as we will see, every invisible truth can manifest from the supernatural to the physical and reach our five physical senses through revelation.

Most of the supernatural manifestations we have seen in the church up to now are the result of God's sovereignty, and not because we have received the revelation to demonstrate that power. I believe that as long as the church lacks revelation, we will not see the demonstrations of the Spirit or the true power of God that are available to us. We need revelation of the biblical knowledge we have gained, of the *logos* Word and the theology we know. This is why the Holy Spirit was sent to us—to reveal those truths and bring visible manifestations of the power of God to the earth.

> ## Revelation of the Word is the place where the Holy Spirit manifests supernatural demonstrations of power.

REVELATION BRINGS THE MANIFESTATION

We need to truly understand that what sets apart the believers who manifest the power of God from those who don't is revelation. Many people embrace supernatural truths such as revival, anointing, the miracles of the Holy Spirit, deliverance, and the gifts, but they don't manifest them because they don't know how. Our generation is desperate not only to hear a message, but also to see the power of God demonstrated. When a church makes excuses for not manifesting His power, it gives birth to believers who have a passive faith. That is why there are so many children of God today who compromise the truth and are more concerned about pleasing people than about knowing Him through the manifestations of His Holy Spirit. Again, my question is, have you let God use you to demonstrate His power—to make a blind person see or a deaf person hear?

The following are some ways in which revelation leads to manifestation:

+ *Revelation loosens spiritual activity.* A person's level of revelation can be measured by the spiritual activity they manifest. This is known as the "mantle of revelation," which God gives to every one of His ministers. When someone carries revelation, they provoke spiritual activity that manifests the presence of God to others. The enemy knows if you are carrying revelation, and he will attack you, sometimes even physically, to stop the growth of that revelation and its manifestation.

+ *Revelation stimulates your thoughts.* When a child of God carries revelation of the Holy Spirit, this is manifested in an increase of their mental abilities.

+ *Revelation transforms people.* If you are not being transformed, it is because you are receiving only information and not revelation.

+ *Revelation accelerates the growth of the people of God.* Revelation produces so much acceleration in the natural that it activates us to walk in the supernatural. It takes us back to our original state as human beings, when God brought Adam to life with the breath of His Spirit. Every time revelation comes into our lives by the impartation of the Holy Spirit, acceleration will manifest in every area of our being.

The level of a leader's revelation will determine the spiritual activity for their church.

5. THE DIFFERENCE BETWEEN KNOWLEDGE AND EXPERIENCE

Jesus promised His disciples a higher level of knowledge and power when He said to them, *"But stay here in the city until the Holy Spirit comes and fills you with power from heaven"* (Luke 24:49 NLT). The *New King James Version* reads, *"…until you are endued with power from on high."* In Greek, the word for *"fills"* or *"endued"* is *enduo*, which also means to be "clothed" with power, including abilities and knowledge.

On the day of Pentecost, God imparted to Jesus' followers not only His power but also His revelation, because He does not allow His power to function with merely carnal or natural information. God's power is for those who want to be witnesses of Jesus, and His knowledge enables us to know how to operate in that power. *"And they went out and preached everywhere, the Lord working with them and confirming the word through the accompanying signs"* (Mark 16:20). The knowledge of God leads us to have an experience with Him and His power through the Holy Spirit.

When God imparts His power, He also gives us His knowledge.

The Word of God is His life force. (See John 1:1, 14; 14:6.) This means that when we receive His Spirit, we also receive His life force— His teachings and the knowledge of *"all things."* (See John 14:26.) When we walk with Him, we don't speak out of our own intelligence; rather, the One who speaks is the Holy Spirit who dwells inside of us. The words we speak are loaded with power because the knowledge of God has led us to an experience with the Spirit. Thus, it is not what we know or how we say something that makes the difference, but rather the Spirit by which we know the truth and by which we speak it. We should not speak out of our own personal opinions, but from the knowledge the Spirit has allowed us to experience.

The human mind tends to reject the experiences of the Spirit because we are programmed in our culture to receive information without having an experience. That is why Jesus *"appeared to the eleven as they sat at the table; and He rebuked their unbelief and hardness of heart, because they did not believe those who had seen Him after He had risen"* (Mark 16:14). Here we see that Jesus had risen from the dead, just as He had promised to His disciples. However, when He met with them, He had to rebuke them because not only had they doubted His word, they had also mocked those who had seen Him after He had risen again. Even when He stood before them, Thomas could barely believe. Things are not much different today. After experiencing the supernatural in our meetings, some people still refuse to change.

One day, I asked one of my assistants, who studied business administration in a prestigious university in Florida, how many of her professors had experience in the business field. Her answer was that none of them did! My question is, why are people teaching how to do business if they don't have any experience with it? The fact is that this kind of thing is very common in Western societies. If someone knows what they need to say and how to say it, it doesn't matter if they have never practiced it. But this is not how the kingdom works! To walk in the principles of God, we need both the knowledge and the experience. In today's church, there are people who have never had an experience with the knowledge they have, and others who are worse off because they don't even have the theory. Both of these groups need an experience!

Knowledge will be genuine only when it is experienced.

The true knowledge I refer to cannot be acquired by reading many books. There are theologians who know the Bible better than the back of their hand, but their spiritual lives are dry. They have memorized the Scriptures from beginning to end, but when it comes time to apply this knowledge, they have no idea how. The problem is that they have studied the letter of the Bible but not the living Word. It is one thing to speak about faith, but another to live by it. That is why they know *about* God, but they don't *know* God.

> **When we have an experience with God's knowledge, we can describe, teach, and impart it with precision and confidence.**

When we lack the experience that complements what we know, we are not being truthful with ourselves or with the Lord. Nearly all the world's religions lack an encounter with their god. However, Christianity offers us that experience. If you are a child of God, washed by the blood of Jesus and filled with the Holy Spirit, you do not have to fear having an experience with Him. The Holy Spirit wants to have an encounter with you to bring life to your knowledge. He wants to give you a real experience, here and now. Do you want to have an encounter with the knowledge of the Spirit?

6. THE DIFFERENCE BETWEEN THE WORD AND THE PRESENCE OF GOD

We have previously defined God's Word as *logos* and *rhema*, and we have seen how people separate teaching from revelation, practice, and experience. Many believers separate the Word from the presence of God because they don't understand that each fulfills a distinct role. The presence of God is His glory manifested in a visible way, here and now. The Word must be preached in the supernatural atmosphere of His presence so that it can be imparted to people's hearts by the power of the resurrection.

The Word is the portion of teaching that every pastor or leader must prepare in order to spiritually feed the people of God. It must be studied and prepared in intimacy with the Lord. That is why we read in Paul's letter to Timothy, "*I charge you therefore before God and the Lord Jesus…: Preach the word! Be ready in season and out of season. Convince, rebuke, exhort, with all longsuffering and teaching*" (2 Timothy 4:1–2). Yet without the presence of God, the Word can be nothing more than a collection of historical texts that will not change the hearts of His people. If the Word of God is preached in a place where His presence is not manifesting, the teaching will be dry. That is why we see so many ministries where there is no manifestation of miracles, no one receives the Lord, people are not transformed, and growth is nonexistent. Though their emphasis is on the Word, the presence of God is not there.

The presence of God in a church is the supernatural manifestation of the Holy Spirit, who shows us—more than do the mind, the emotions, and the natural senses—the existence of God. His presence carries the power to give life, transform, heal, and provide for the needs of each member of the congregation. We are called to worship the Lord in our services so that He may manifest Himself and touch the hearts of the people to receive His Word. The presence of God should manifest in every service, as well as in our personal time with the Father. (See, for example, 2 Chronicles 7:1–2.)

When I go somewhere to preach, and I perceive that the presence of God is not there, I begin to seek Him, to cry out for His presence, and to manifest that presence, because I know that without Him, I cannot impart the Word to anyone effectively. If His presence is already there, then I will work with the particular aspect of truth He is manifesting.

Today, the challenge is to teach and train people to learn how to bring God's presence to earth. For the presence of God to manifest in and among us, we need to respond to Him and what He is going to do in that moment. The following verse tells of a particular moment in Jesus' ministry when God's presence was there: "*Now it happened on a certain day, as He was teaching, that there were Pharisees and teachers of the law sitting by, who had come out of every town of Galilee, Judea, and Jerusalem. And the power of the Lord was present to heal them"* (Luke 5:17). Curiously, only one miracle happened at that time, because the people did not receive the power or the presence of God in Jesus.

The manifest presence is heaven's provision for the *now*—not for the "later." Whenever His presence becomes strong during a service, that is the time to stop preaching and give complete control to the Holy Spirit. The message can be preached any time, but when God is present, we must give room to the Holy Spirit and let His will be done. Many times, I have had to interrupt my message and continue it in the next service, or even later in the week, to yield to God so He may do whatever He wants to do at that time with His people.

Words cannot replace actions, or actions replace words; both are necessary to demonstrate the power of God.

7. THE DIFFERENCE BETWEEN WORDS AND WORKS

At the beginning of the book of Acts, the author speaks about the purpose for which he wrote the gospel of Luke, saying, *"The former account I made, O Theophilus, of all that Jesus began both to do and teach…"* (Acts 1:1). It was clear to Luke that Jesus' ministry consisted of both teachings and works. Unfortunately, these days, we have affirmed the teaching while putting the works aside because we are afraid of demonstrating what we preach, or of praying and not seeing any manifestation. This did not happen with Jesus because He *"was a Prophet mighty **in deed and word** before God and all the people"* (Luke 24:19). Jesus spoke about the same thing when He said, *"Believe Me that I am in the Father and the Father in Me, or else believe Me for the sake of the works themselves"* (John 14:11). It is not enough to have the right words; we need the actions, the concrete works, corresponding to what we preach. It is when people see the manifest proof that many will believe that Jesus is the Messiah, the Son of God. (See John 20:30–31.)

DEMONSTRATING THE SPIRIT AND HIS POWER

To implement what I have been describing in this chapter, we must affirm where God's power dwells, so that we can see the manifestations of His Spirit—supernatural power is connected to both a knowledge of the Word and the presence of God. Wherever there is revealed knowledge, there is power to demonstrate.

To demonstrate is to manifest or show that something is true with unquestionable evidence, to confirm with clear proof the things of which we speak. A demonstration is not a theory, a philosophical trend, or words that stay in the realm of ideas or mental knowledge. It goes above and beyond rationality and intelligence because God Himself testifies with us. (See Hebrews 2:4.) The Holy Spirit gives us His power so that we can give unquestionable proof of His existence and of the sacrifice of Jesus and the power He released on the cross for humanity. The miracles are what draw people closer to Him to be saved, healed, and transformed, and bring the kingdom of heaven to earth.

As has been expressed, many of us make the mistake of preaching Jesus and His kingdom without the demonstration of power. In his first letter to the Corinthians, the apostle Paul spoke about the importance of demonstration for establishing people's faith in the power of God:

And I, brethren, when I came to you, did not come with excellence of speech or of wisdom declaring to you the testimony of God. For I determined not to know anything among you except Jesus Christ and Him crucified. I was with you in weakness, in fear, and in much trembling. And my speech and my preaching were not with persuasive words of human wisdom, but in demonstration of the Spirit and

*of power, that your faith should not be in the wisdom of men but in
the power of God.* (1 Corinthians 2:1–5)

Here Paul recognized his failure of trying to impress the people in
Athens, the summit of wisdom at that time, with a message of human
wisdom instead of walking in the power of the cross. (See Acts 17:16–
32.) During that trip, he learned how *not* to preach the gospel of the kingdom. That is why, before going to Corinth, he prepared himself to preach
"Jesus Christ and Him crucified" (1 Corinthians 2:2) and to demonstrate
the Word with the move of the Spirit and the power of God.

Manifestations of the power of God are that which can be captured
by our five senses. For example, the blind can receive their sight, the deaf
can receive their hearing, those oppressed by demons can be set free and
experience release from bondage, and those confined to a wheelchair for
years can be healed and walk again, all by the power and love of God. All
of these are demonstrations that can be witnessed and confirmed. When
His power is demonstrated, we see tangible proof of the Spirit of the
Lord. That means both the person of the Holy Spirit and His supernatural power can be demonstrated in the here and now. This happens when
we surrender to the Holy Spirit because *"the manifestation of the Spirit is
given to each one for the profit of all"* (1 Corinthians 12:7).

A demonstration is a visible manifestation, open to the five senses.

Concerning this point, I must repeat that God never authorized the
church to preach the gospel without demonstrating His power. *"For the
kingdom of God is not in word but in power"* (1 Corinthians 4:20). On

the contrary, the Lord's blueprint for revealing Himself to us has always consisted of a manifestation of supernatural power.

Let us confirm this truth with other portions of Scripture. When Moses went to Pharaoh to tell him to release God's people from slavery, he did so with demonstrations of God's power. (See, for example, Exodus 8.) When Joseph revealed the meaning of Pharaoh's dream, he did so by the power of the Spirit. (See Genesis 41:16, 28, 38.) When Elijah defeated the four hundred and fifty prophets of Baal, he did so after calling down fire from heaven in the power of God. (See 1 Kings 18:20–40.) There is no one in the Bible who was sent out by the Lord who did not demonstrate His supernatural power. The Spirit and His power will manifest here and now if we know how to walk in them. This was the case with Jesus' personal disciples when *"they went out and preached everywhere, the Lord working with them and confirming the word through the accompanying signs"* (Mark 16:20).

The supernatural power of God is in His Word and His truth.

THE CONDITION FOR DEMONSTRATING THE SPIRIT AND HIS POWER

Thus, we must understand that before the power of God comes upon us, it is first found in His Word. We have seen that when God sends His word and someone receives it through revelation, He backs it up with His power. He promised, *"So shall My word be that goes forth from My mouth; it shall not return to Me void, but it shall accomplish what I please, and it shall prosper in the thing for which I sent it"* (Isaiah 55:11). The Word works for every believer, and the signs will follow everyone who believes in the Scriptures and gives the Holy Spirit the freedom to work in their lives.

Every spiritual reality should be demonstrated in the natural. If what we preach is truly revelation, it should manifest. We ought to be people who demonstrate what we say and believe. It is easy to speak about things that cannot be demonstrated, or have not been experienced, because our credibility is not at risk. For example, it is easy to say a quick prayer and ask for someone's healing without really expecting anything to happen.

The condition for manifesting supernatural power is the revelation of knowledge. Without a demonstration, the revelation has no credibility.

We have gotten used to valuing concepts above experiences and demonstrations. One reason for this is that some people have been deceived by false experiences, and they don't want to be deceived again, so they pull back from the supernatural. But they are missing out on the reality of genuine supernatural revelation and demonstrations from the Holy Spirit.

THE NEED AND IMPORTANCE OF DEMONSTRATING THE SPIRIT AND HIS POWER

God wants to have an encounter with you, and that encounter should take place in the spiritual and manifest in the natural. God is not a mere concept or an idea; He is a Person. Every revelation we receive from His Spirit leads us to a divine encounter through which we can draw closer to Him and drink deeply of His presence. The Lord does not give us revelation just so we can have more knowledge in our heads. It is so we can have an experience, a divine encounter, with Him and become true witnesses of Jesus. Are you ready to have an encounter with the Holy Spirit? Then this is the time. Our generation wants to see the manifestation of His power so they can believe.

> **Yes, you can be deceived by a false experience. But if you don't have any experience, you are already deceived!**

Here are the chief reasons we need to demonstrate the power of the Spirit:

+ To show that Jesus Christ is alive in the now. (See, for example, Acts 3:11–16; 2 Corinthians 4:10–11.)

+ To demonstrate that Jesus never changes; He is the same yesterday, today, and forever. (See Hebrews 13:8.)

+ Because the power proves that Jesus will return. (See Acts 1:11.) Supernatural signs always point to a higher reality, and every sign, wonder, and miracle we manifest points to His second coming.

+ To confirm that the Word of God is true. (See, for example, 2 Samuel 7:28; John 17:17.)

+ Because the power proves God's integrity. (See, for example, Numbers 23:19; Mark 16:20.)

+ Because the power confronts and subjugates Satan; it is the proof that his occupation on earth has ended and the government of God has been established. The kingdom of God pushes out the enemy and his kingdom of darkness wherever they seek to gain control. (See, for example, Luke 10:19; 11:20; 1 John 3:8.)

A demonstration of power makes us credible witnesses of the kingdom gospel. We must demonstrate what we preach if we want our message to be heard. This means that when someone does not demonstrate what they preach, their message is not trustworthy. If a lawyer presents a witness to testify in court, the first requirement is to make sure the person has seen, heard, or otherwise had a firsthand experience with what they are testifying about. The more direct and personal their testimony, the more believable it is and the stronger its foundation of truth. This is why, if you have never experienced the power of God, you are not a credible witness of what you preach; you are just repeating what you have heard others say. The reality of the Spirit must be seen in the natural; otherwise, people will always believe in something other than the true gospel.

More and more people of God are demanding that every preacher, pastor, and leader demonstrate what they teach. Unfortunately, we have reduced the message of God's kingdom to simply the forgiveness of sins, even though the good news of salvation includes all of the perfect plan of God for mankind and the lordship of Jesus Christ. Jesus said, *"Repent, and believe in the gospel"* (Mark 1:15). This means that repentance of sins is the first part, but immediately afterward it tells us to believe in the gospel. But in what gospel? The gospel *of the kingdom*. (See, for example, Matthew 4:23; Luke 8:1.) The good news of the kingdom goes beyond the salvation of the soul and includes demonstrations of power through healings, deliverance, financial blessings, and breakthroughs in every area of life. It is complete redemption for every son and daughter of Christ, and leads us to the original purpose of God.

THE RISK OF MANIFESTING THE SPIRIT OF GOD AND HIS POWER

We cannot expect God to show us His power by accident. Instead, it is our duty to create the conditions for His presence and power to flow.

In our ministry, we have created a safe environment for people to learn how to demonstrate the power of God. They can make mistakes as they go through the process of developing their spiritual senses, establishing an intimate relationship with God, and walking in the power of the Holy Spirit. I have often had to correct them, but I never publicly humiliate or mistreat people. My desire is for everyone to move with boldness in the dimension of the Spirit so that the Lord may use them in miracles and healings. If they were reproached each time they made a small mistake, they would never feel secure, and that would interfere with their development. I have a responsibility to train and equip them to grow in their spiritual leadership.

The only way to reach a higher dimension is by learning from your mistakes.

Through this spiritual training, hundreds of leaders have gone out from our church. Countless men and women have learned how to hear the voice of God and obey it, people who flow in the same spirit with me and help me to minister, without quenching or grieving the Holy Spirit. Many of them have gone on to build churches, both in the United States and in other parts of the world. Others have remained in Miami, helping to train the new generations of leaders there whom God is using for His purposes.

The church of Jesus today needs more "Peters"—people who dare to step out of the boat by faith!

And Peter answered [Jesus] and said, "Lord, if it is You, command me to come to You on the water." So He said, "Come." And when

Peter had come down out of the boat, he walked on the water to go to Jesus. But when he saw that the wind was boisterous, he was afraid; and beginning to sink he cried out, saying, "Lord, save me!" And immediately Jesus stretched out His hand and caught him, and said to him, "O you of little faith, why did you doubt?"

(Matthew 14:28–31)

The power of God does not activate by coincidence, but with purpose.

Most people who read these verses remember only the part about how Peter sank. They ignore the fact that he was the only one who dared to step out of the boat, while the rest were bound by fear. He challenged himself and his faith to go to the next level in his spiritual progress, and we should dare to do the same, walking in the things God has for us. Take risks! If the Lord tells you to pray for a sick person, do it! If He says to cast out demons, do it! Sometimes we avoid taking risks because we don't want to place our reputation on the line, but we need to learn to trust God.

As I write this book, I again feel the need to lead people to an encounter and an experience with the living God, and not just to teach a nice message. I believe we have reduced the gospel to mere positive teachings, removing its power. However, it is time to show the truth of these teachings and give the world an experience with the Father. I refuse to conform! I want to go beyond simple preaching and give people visible demonstrations of the power of God, to heal and deliver as Jesus did.

Again, it is easier to offer friendly prayers and not expect anything to occur than to take the risk of praying for something supernatural to happen. But how can we say we love our neighbors and not do anything about their needs?

Walking in faith is a risk, but walking with God is never a risk.

By this we know love, because He laid down His life for us. And we also ought to lay down our lives for the brethren. But whoever has this world's goods, and sees his brother in need, and shuts up his heart from him, how does the love of God abide in him?

(1 John 3:16–17)

The faith that comes from God leaves no room for doubt. That faith simply is, because God is. Are you walking in faith and taking risks? If not, then you need to receive God's boldness. Dare to be bold, be willing to do what makes you appear ridiculous, and visualize the impossible. Throughout His ministry, Jesus took great risks, like the time He demonstrated the gospel of the kingdom by healing a paralytic man through the forgiveness of his sins: *"'But that you may know that the Son of Man has power on earth to forgive sins'—then He said to the paralytic, 'Arise, take up your bed, and go to your house'"* (Matthew 9:6).

With this miracle, Jesus revealed that He was the "Son of Man," the Messiah. He basically told the paralyzed man, "I am the Messiah and I have power, so take up your bed and walk." If this man had not gotten up, Jesus would have been in trouble. However, His faith was absolute, and He was willing to risk it all, starting with His identity and reputation.

This is how confident He was in the support and power of the Father upon Him.

As for you, are you willing to put your reputation on the line? Are you tired of messages without demonstration? Are you bored of much theory but no practice? Does it bother you to hear the Word without the presence of God? Do you believe the Bible is not just a storybook but something whose truths you can experience? Are you willing to step out of the boat and walk upon the waters? Are you ready to pray for the sick and cast out demons? Remember that the power of God is based on the truth, and it works for all who walk in the truth. Miracles, signs, and wonders should follow every believer, not because of their fame or personality but because the truth dwells in them.

> ## Our God is a God of power, and we need to demonstrate that today.

Thousands of people from every part of the world come to my meetings and Supernatural Encounters to be changed and transformed forever by the power of God. You can be, too. The Spirit of God is waiting for you to surrender to Him and give Him room to work in your life. He is waiting for you to say, "Yes, Holy Spirit, use me as a vessel to heal the sick and cast out demons, starting with my family and myself." There are many people who don't accept the Lord because they are still waiting to see His manifest presence. As children of God, we owe people an experience with the Father. Again, it is not only about the letter of the Word. We need its power! I pray for the Holy Spirit to bring you revelation so you can walk in the supernatural of God.

Personally, I can share many testimonies of times in my life when I had to take great risks to demonstrate God's power. For example, some years ago, I was invited to a presidential breakfast in Washington, DC, and I was seated next to a government official. I noticed he was using hearing aids and asked if I could pray for him. I did this in front of a lot of people, even George W. Bush, who was president at the time. I took a risk, God backed me up, and the man's ears were healed.

On another occasion, I was preaching at a conference in Ukraine and I announced that I would manifest the five miracles of the kingdom: the blind would see, the deaf would hear, the mute would speak, the lame would walk, and demons would be cast out. I gave an altar call for those who needed to be healed and delivered, prayed for many people, and demonstrated the power of God in front of everyone there. When they saw these miracles, many people came to the feet of Jesus, because when the power is demonstrated through supernatural works, people believe.

It is easy to speak of something we have not experienced when our credibility is not at risk.

Today, many preachers pray for people, but they don't ask for testimonies because they are afraid that no one will respond. They do not prophesy or give words of knowledge out of fear that nothing will happen and they will ruin their reputations. Do you know how many times I have prayed and nothing has happened? I have lost count! Other times, I have prayed and only one person has been healed. But I have persevered. I believe that the Word of God is the truth, and my reason for demonstrating the power of the Holy Spirit is not to be famous but to exalt the name of Jesus. I encourage you today to take a leap of faith. Be bold, and demonstrate the power of God!

At an opportune moment, my son Bryan, while returning from a trip, stood up in an airplane and began preaching the gospel and praying for people. He took a risk, not caring what they thought of him. This is the generation that God is raising; so be bold and take risks for Him. You have to die to self and believe that when you walk in faith, God will manifest the Spirit to you and through you. If He doesn't do it, then you need to continue to die to self and keep believing until something happens. When God sees that you are dead to yourself, He will start doing great things through you. Are you willing to demonstrate the Spirit? This is the time and this is the generation that is expecting a great demonstration of power!

> **We cannot claim a spiritual reality without showing its evidence in the natural; that is why we need to demonstrate what we say and believe.**

ACTIVATION

Pray this prayer in faith:

Beloved Spirit of God, today I have received Your Word, and I feel that You are calling me to a new level of intimacy in my walk with You. I need You to open my understanding so that I may know the difference between the *logos* and the *rhema*, between the written Word and Your spoken word for today, between the Word and the works, between theory and practice, between revelation and manifestation, between knowledge and experience. Help me to know Your Word and Your presence, and how they complement each other.

Holy Spirit, I need to be activated in You, to demonstrate Your power to this generation that loves knowledge but rejects a supernatural experience with a supernatural God. Father, I am Your child, and I want to manifest Your power as I walk through life, whether in school, at work, on vacation, or anywhere else. Confirm Your Word, Your truth, and Your revelation with miracles, signs, and wonders. Lord, help me to give this world an experience with You. Holy Spirit, impart Your boldness to me to shake me from my comfort zone so that I dare to take risks, to pray for the sick, to prophesy, to cast out demons, and to move in Your gifts. I know that You will support me in Your words and truth. If I make mistakes in the process, I know You are faithful to forgive me and to give me the grace to keep risking my reputation, as long as I see Your power being manifested here and now. Amen.

6

HOW TO BE CONTINUOUSLY
FILLED WITH THE HOLY SPIRIT

We men and women of the twenty-first century are living in difficult times. Crime and violence impact everything around us, and we frequently experience natural disasters such as earthquakes, droughts, floods, fires, tornadoes, and more. At the human level, we see new diseases, addictions, emotional disorders, and broken families. At the societal level, we see crises in the economy, government, and business, along with the effects of dueling theories and paradigms such as postmodernism, in which most established values are questioned. Many people today refuse to accept the fact that there are absolute truths because they have been deceived by the promotion of various political and social agendas.

In the midst of this scenario, Christians need to be filled with the Holy Spirit more than ever before. This is the only way to overpower sin and conquer evil in a world that is in crisis. It is the only weapon we have to defend ourselves against temptations and our flesh, and to defeat the enemy; any other way would be impossible.

WHAT DOES IT MEAN TO BE FILLED WITH THE HOLY SPIRIT?

Nowadays, many churches teach a theology that emphasizes spiritual tongues but neglects the power of God. I speak in tongues, and in our church all the believers receive the baptism with the Holy Spirit with the evidence of speaking in other tongues. (See Acts 2:4.) However, we know that God's desire is not just for us to speak in tongues, but also to manifest the power of the Holy Spirit. Tongues are only the indication that the Spirit of God has come into our lives so that we can testify about the risen Christ with power. Jesus said, *"But you shall receive power when the Holy Spirit has come upon you; and you shall be witnesses to Me in Jerusalem, and in all Judea and Samaria, and to the end of the earth"* (Acts 1:8).

Certain Christian groups have made a particular theology out of this verse, saying that being filled with the Holy Spirit happens just once and that is enough. However it is interesting to see that in the second chapter of the book of Acts, the apostles first *"were all filled with the Holy Spirit and began to speak with other tongues, as the Spirit gave them utterance"* (Acts 2:4). Then, in the fourth chapter, we see that *"when they had prayed, the place where they were assembled together was shaken; and they were all filled with the Holy Spirit, and they spoke the word of God with boldness"* (Acts 4:31). They were filled with the Holy Spirit again. This shows an ongoing need to be filled with the Spirit in order to fulfill what God has called us to do.

It is true that there is only one baptism in the Holy Spirit because this is a unique experience. However, one must ask, how long does the initial infilling last? If the disciples had already received the baptism and been filled, why did they have to be filled again? The answer is simple: There is no spiritual filling that lasts forever, at least on this earth; it is an experience that must be repeated regularly. We need to be continually filled because the Lord wants to continue doing His work through us. That is why we see in Acts 13:52 that *"the disciples were filled with joy and with the Holy Spirit."*

> ## The baptism of the Holy Spirit happens once, but being filled should be repeated as many times as we need it.

You cannot overcome and be relevant in today's world with yesterday's anointing. Yesterday's faith does not work for today. This means your spirit should always be saturated with the presence of God and remain in the atmosphere of the supernatural, because from there flows the manifest presence of the Father, and it is there where the Holy Spirit moves with freedom and power. This way, you will always be ready to exercise the power of God, which is first received when we are baptized in the Holy Spirit.

After Jesus ascended to heaven, Peter and John went to pray at the synagogue and found a man who had been paralyzed since birth, begging at its door. The man asked them for charity, and *"then Peter said, 'Silver and gold I do not have, but what I do have I give you: In the name of Jesus Christ of Nazareth, rise up and walk.' And he took him by the right hand and lifted him up, and immediately his feet and ankle bones received strength"* (Acts 3:6–7). Here we see that Peter was in a supernatural state and used the power of God that was already stored within him to heal the lame man; he did not have to struggle to produce the miracle. And this is how every believer should be—super-naturalized! If every believer walked a life continually filled with the Holy Spirit, miracles would be a regular occurrence.

The problem is not so much filling believers with the Holy Spirit, but keeping them filled.

Most pastors minister to people in the areas where those individuals are the most empty of the Holy Spirit. The ministers have to pray for them over and over again because wherever we are not filled with the Spirit, we are not free. If you are filled with the Holy Spirit, there is no room for anything negative or harmful. But where the overflow of the Spirit runs out and is not replenished, the old man (the flesh and the "self") and the enemy begin to occupy the empty places. Your walk with God becomes religious; you easily return to the letter of the Word, of the law, and of faith. You have lost the Spirit of the Word, and your faith has become mechanical. You may speak in tongues, but it will be like "a clanging cymbal" (see 1 Corinthians 13:1); you will become someone who merely repeats the same tongues because that is what you have memorized. You can dance and jump because you know the steps, but it will be without power because the Holy Spirit is not there.

How can someone be filled with the Holy Spirit and have room for anything else? If there is something else, we need to know how it got there. There must be no room in us for bad thoughts, doubt, confusion, or disbelief. We must not be full of ourselves, our flesh, and hatred, or other feelings that are not of God. If we are filled with the love of money, lust, pride, or knowledge, we are empty of the Holy Spirit, and we have given place to the natural.

THE DIFFERENCE BETWEEN SPIRIT BAPTISM AND BEING FILLED WITH THE SPIRIT

Let's consider further what it means to be baptized with the Spirit compared to what it means to be filled with the Spirit. To be baptized with the Holy Spirit means being saturated with or submerged in the miraculous power of God. When one is baptized with the Spirit, it is not that the individual has a lot of God, but that God has that individual in the river of His Spirit. This means there is no limitation in baptism.

On the other hand, being "filled" refers to being at maximum capacity. Thus, to be filled with the Holy Spirit means to contain the highest measure of God possible. We are God's vessels, and it is our purpose to hold the presence of the Lord inside us and to be transformed forever in the process. In this case, it is us having God, rather than Him having us. That is why there is a limit to the fullness or measure of God we can contain, and why the measure can decrease.

> ## Whatever you are not dead to will expose the areas where you are empty of God.

I will give you an example. When you fill your car's gas tank, it is because you expect to use it, and while you are driving from one place to another, you understand that the fuel is being consumed. When you notice that you have only a little fuel left in the tank, you stop at a gas station and add more. The gas tank has a limited amount of storage, so regardless of how often you fill it up, you will eventually have to add to it again. In the same way, the Holy Spirit fills us with a certain amount of God's presence and gives us supernatural power to operate with the same anointing and revelation as the Father, and to do the works of Jesus. We should expect to use that anointing and to understand that we will need to be filled again when we do.

In the past, there were movements of the Spirit where people did not understand the difference between being baptized and being filled. However, we need the two types of experiences because, again, even though we are baptized with the Holy Spirit and have been submerged under His miraculous power, we need to be continually filled by the Holy Spirit throughout our lives. This filling depends on a permanent relationship with God that we must maintain by pursuing Him and His Spirit.

When we begin to walk with Christ, we can be filled with the Spirit even without having been baptized with Him. In fact, I believe that today's church has become stagnant by concentrating on the fullness while remaining ignorant about the baptism. What position do you find yourself in? Have you been baptized with the Spirit? Have you been filled with Him? Many Christians know the Holy Spirit and are filled with Him, but they have not been baptized. The New Testament describes being saved, baptized, and filled. The apostles understood all three stages.

In Luke 24:49, just before His ascension, Jesus told His disciples to wait in Jerusalem for the Father's promise of *"power from on high."* However, prior to this, He gathered His disciples and *"breathed on them, and said to them, 'Receive the Holy Spirit'"* (John 20:22). This was the first breath of the Spirit, by which they were saved and born again. It was when the disciples saw and believed that Jesus had been raised from the dead that He breathed the Spirit into them. This means that you are not saved until you accept the death and resurrection of Jesus on your behalf, and receive forgiveness for your sins. Second, we see in the book of Acts that Jesus' disciples were baptized with the fire of the Holy Spirit; they were clothed with power from above. (See Acts 2.) And third, as we have noted, they were filled again with the Spirit.

WHY WE NEED TO BE CONTINUALLY FILLED

Personally, I know that I could not have accomplished everything God has asked of me without being regularly filled with His Spirit. That is why I must continually seek Him. If time passes without my receiving something new from Him, I feel a terrible need. This need is a reality for all who are not yet replenished by the Spirit.

In Acts 3:6, Peter told the paralyzed man, *"What I **do have** I give you...."* He was filled with the Holy Spirit, through whom he ministered. Again, the reason why people need continual deliverance and counseling is that they are empty of the Holy Spirit. Paul warned the Ephesians, *"Do not get drunk with wine, for that is wickedness (corruption, stupidity), but be filled with the [Holy] Spirit and constantly guided by Him"* (Ephesians 5:18 AMP).

A lack of fullness of the Holy Spirit produces in us...

+ *Unproductivity.* When we are not filled with the Holy Spirit, we become unproductive for the kingdom because we lack the power to manifest what we preach. We might speak and teach, but there is no demonstration.

+ *Spiritual leaking.* When we hold on to an offense or carry unforgiveness in our hearts, we quickly lose our fullness. It is as if there is a hole in the bottom of our spiritual deposit. The anointing of the Spirit "leaks," and we lose the power of His presence.

+ *Constant spiritual warfare.* When we are not filled with the Holy Spirit, the enemy uses the empty parts in us—such as the areas of our finances, health, and family—to attack us. As a result, we find ourselves in constant spiritual warfare, struggling against principalities and powers, being tempted and fighting against the flesh, instead of living in the victory we are supposed to have. We fight in our own strength, without the supernatural power that leads us to overcome regardless of the odds.

+ *Naturalization.* A natural man cannot overcome the devil and the impossible circumstances in his life by himself; that is why he needs a power greater than he. When we lose the fullness of the Holy Spirit, we walk in the natural and cannot manifest the supernatural realm of the Spirit.

+ *A loss of what is not used.* The fullness of the Holy Spirit is like the manna that fed the people of Israel daily in the desert. Remember that the manna from one day would not work for another (the only exception being the Sabbath Day). What wasn't eaten would be lost. In the same way, what we don't use when we are filled with the Spirit will be lost.

+ *A return to the world and sin.* As we have seen, when we are not filled with the Spirit, the old nature begins to rise again and start filling the empty spots in our mind, emotions, and will. Little by little, our character starts to backslide, and we return to whatever our life was filled with before; sin no longer seems as terrible to us, and we are in danger of returning to the life of the world.

To overcome all these things, we must spend time with the Holy Spirit until our cup is once again full of His presence.

While we serve God, we will always have the need to be filled and to remain filled with Him.

We can summarize two main reasons why we must always be filled with the Spirit. Because of these reasons, we should be seeking the Lord all the time.

The first reason is in order to live in a constant state of the supernatural, saturated and energized with the power of God. Being full of the Spirit is the state of those who manifest the kingdom of heaven on earth, making them better witnesses for Christ. When people see the fruit of the Spirit in us—love, joy, peace, longsuffering, kindness, goodness, faithfulness, gentleness, and self-control—they know there is something different about our lives. (See Galatians 5:22–23.) They can perceive that we live in victory, even in a world that fights daily against defeat and discouragement, and this makes them desire to have what we have.

The second reason is to demonstrate the power of God wherever we go. If you are not filled with the Spirit, you will not feel the needs of others, nor will your heart be moved to compassion to help them. On the contrary, you will be more interested in satisfying your flesh or the cravings of your old nature. But being full of the Spirit gives us the compassion of Jesus and enables us to demonstrate the power of God. When we pray for the sick and cast out demons, we use the power we initially received when we were baptized in the Holy Spirit and fire, and we also give out of what has been poured into us by the Spirit because we operate from that fullness.

I can give you many examples of how God has demonstrated His power through me as I have prayed for people inside and outside of the church—in parking lots, on airplanes, in restaurants, and elsewhere. Wherever there is a need, I am ready to pray and manifest the power of God. Many people have been healed and delivered instantly because I am continually filled with the Spirit, and I can release His power whenever I want and wherever I go. The same thing will happen for any believer who remains filled with the Spirit and knows how to operate the power they carry.

During the most recent Supernatural Encounter I held in the Arena Ciudad in the capital of Mexico, God told me that the heavens were open and that His Spirit would move with power and miracles. Over twenty thousand people were gathered that day, and in the middle of the supernatural atmosphere more than a dozen people who had arrived in wheelchairs walked toward the altar to give their testimonies of what God had done. Among them, a man named Sabino had this testimony of a powerful healing:

"For forty years, I suffered from septic arthritis, septic shock, and sepsis (a sickness resulting from a grave response to bacteria). I had been left hopeless nearly six months ago. I had gone through six surgeries, and after every operation the doctors told my parents I was dying, that I had only a few minutes left. And every time, my father would go to the hospital chapel and pray. My mother would walk around the operating room, fighting against the spirit of death and declaring life into me. I would come out alive, but I remained sick. This happened during every operation, until four months ago when I went into intensive therapy, and the doctors told my parents they would euthanize me so I could at least die painlessly. Once again, my father and mother went into spiritual warfare, and I came out of the hospital alive, but I could barely move. My parents had to feed me, and I needed help to go to the bathroom.

"My parents took me from the city of Puebla to the Federal District (an hour and a half away) to the Supernatural Encounter. I was in a wheelchair, but when I was prayed for, I felt a strong warmth traveling throughout my whole body. I still don't know how I got up from my wheelchair, but I remember saying, 'I won't sit in it. I am going to push my own wheelchair!' I started walking on my own, and I pushed my wheelchair up to the altar to share my testimony. And as I walked to the platform, the Lord started to heal me!"

Here is another testimony from that Supernatural Encounter that made a strong impression on me. Victor, a Mexican journalist deeply involved in witchcraft, made a choice to stop criticizing the move of God and surrender before His supernatural power.

"Some time ago, I saw Apostle Maldonado preaching on TV, and I thought he was crazy. So, when I found out he would be coming to Mexico, I asked to be sent to cover the event. I requested total access because I wanted to show that the Mexico Supernatural Encounter was a show, that Apostle Maldonado was a liar, and that the testimonies he presented were false. However, as he preached, the Lord healed me of Parkinson's. Because of the disease, I could barely walk, got dizzy spells frequently, couldn't sleep, and could barely go to the bathroom. I had no peace! The doctors told me I would need treatment for the rest of my life. Desperate and without God, I fell into witchcraft, Santeria, voodoo, and the occult. I spent a lot of money traveling to Miami, Cuba, Haiti, and many other places in search of healing. However, on the night of the Encounter, the Spirit of God came over me, healed me of every sickness, and delivered me from witchcraft. That day I understood that regardless of my degrees and achievements, I remained ignorant. God is the only and almighty One!"

The same day, I also heard a testimony from Ana Silvia, who had been suffering for eight years due to trigeminal neuralgia, an illness that causes the nerves to swell, in turn affecting the face, eyes, and neck, causing intense pain. This is what she told me:

"No one could touch me, not even softly, because it would produce extreme pain and electric waves throughout my body. The doctors told me the sickness had no cure; it could only be mildly controlled. Although at times the pain is due to inflammation in certain parts of the brain, in the majority of cases there isn't an identifiable cause.

"I traveled from Salamanca, Guanajuato, to Mexico City, with the expectation that God was going to heal me. When they prayed for me, I felt heat going through my body, and I was completely healed! Now, you can touch me and I don't feel the electric waves! Thank you, Father God!"

If you receive the revelation in this book and seek the continual filling of the Holy Spirit, you are ready to demonstrate the power of God whenever and wherever you go. Pray for someone who is sick, and they will be healed; pray for someone living in depression, and they will be set free. For every difficult situation that the enemy attacks you with, you will overcome if you operate from a supernatural atmosphere. You will advance the kingdom of God, expanding it wherever you go, because you will be filled with the Spirit of the Lord.

WHAT ARE THE REQUIREMENTS FOR BEING CONTINUOUSLY FILLED WITH THE HOLY SPIRIT?

Perhaps you are asking yourself what you need to do to be filled with the Spirit of God. You may wonder, *Does the Holy Spirit pour out His presence only to some people or to everyone?* and *Is there something I need to seek?* There are certain conditions for the fullness of the Holy Spirit to become a constant part of your lifestyle and for the power of God to be with you wherever you go.

1. RECOGNIZE YOUR SPIRITUAL CONDITION

Many people fail to have an encounter with the Spirit of God because they ignore the fact that they need one. If someone does not recognize their needy condition, they cannot be filled with the Spirit. Acknowledging what we need gives Him room to move freely in our lives.

Knowing our spiritual condition also leads us to renounce everything taking up space in our hearts and minds that belongs to the Holy Spirit. To empty ourselves is to renounce every distraction, human effort, vice, sin, apathy, and so forth that is cluttering and smothering our lives. This means we must empty ourselves and cry out to the Holy Spirit, so that He knows He is welcome within us.

In our ministry, the leadership and the congregation are frequently exposed to a fresh outpouring of the love and presence of the Father. I know I cannot demand my leaders to operate in the supernatural if their spirits are not filled with God. As their spiritual father, I make sure to minister that fullness, and teach them to depend on the Spirit.

2. BE HUNGRY AND THIRSTY FOR GOD

Jesus gave this invitation to those who are thirsty for God:

Now on the last and most important day of the feast, Jesus stood and called out [in a loud voice], "If anyone is thirsty, let him come to Me and drink! He who believes in Me [who adheres to, trusts in, and relies on Me], as the Scripture has said, 'From his innermost being will flow continually rivers of living water.'" But He was speaking of the [Holy] Spirit, whom those who believed in Him [as Savior] were to receive afterward. The Spirit had not yet been given, because Jesus was not yet glorified (raised to honor). (John 7:37–39 AMP)

Whether we acknowledge it or not, we will become spiritually dehydrated if we do not continue to drink of the waters of eternal life. (See John 4:10.) Sometimes, when we have abundance in the natural—success, riches, popularity, good looks, and so on—we stop thirsting for God. We think that what we received yesterday is enough for today, and that the fullness we receive today is enough for tomorrow. This is wrong! We must pursue God more each day. The impossibilities we and others constantly face show us that we must be filled with His presence at all times.

The Lord will not fill anyone who does not hunger and thirst for Him. Hunger and thirst for His presence make you go after God in order to know Him and receive more of His presence. When you stop being hungry and thirsty for Him, you become irrelevant and long for the person you used to be before you knew God. You start doing things you never would have done when you were walking closely with God, like compromising your principles, because your spiritual desire has diminished. You are separated from God more and more every day, and you are empty of what only the Father can give.

Hunger and thirst come before eating and drinking.

Thus, the condition for Him to cause a deep change in your heart is a hunger and thirst for Him. You must feel, *I need the Holy Spirit*, and mean it so strongly that you depend completely on Him. Hunger makes you go after God beyond what is normal for you; it causes you to seek Him beyond the familiar, comfortable, convenient, or safe. If you don't feel that need, no one can force you to eat and drink of Him.

In the natural, you know when you need to eat or drink because your body sends you signals. In the spiritual, it is more subtle, but there are signs. Unfortunately, we often ignore them, thinking we don't need more of the Holy Spirit, because we are full of those things that are vain and superficial. The Lord cannot give more to someone who is satisfied with where they are. If you are content merely reading about God or seeing how He uses other people in miracles and prophecy; if a simple message once a week on Sunday is enough for you; if you are satisfied with having a religion and living in tradition, then the Holy Spirit cannot fill you.

Remember that spiritual hunger and thirst increase our capacity to receive from God. When someone hungers and thirsts for the Lord, they feel as though they will never have enough. There comes a time when they are full and cannot receive anymore, but soon they will become hungry and thirsty again and desire to be refilled. How can we know when someone is hungry and thirsty for the presence of God? People who long for God are always praying, fasting, worshipping, praising, sowing, and giving to others.

A thirsty person will seek God.

I believe we must seek God more, because in the end what He wants is to demonstrate His love and power through us. The Holy Spirit wants to use us as vessels He can fill to the brim. Vessels who are full of the power of God are the ones who will go out in the name of Jesus to heal the sick and deliver the oppressed. I will show you this principle through testimonies of what God has done through my ministry. This past year, during the thirty-day fast that our whole church participated in, before our yearly leadership summit called the Apostolic and Prophetic

Conference (CAP), the Lord was very specific and told me He would perform many creative miracles. He told me He had ordered the angels to bring new body parts for those who were missing organs, so I activated the people to receive a wave of miracles. Creative miracles took place in the midst of a people who were hungry and thirsty to see the Lord manifest with power. The following are just a few examples of what happened.

Hunger and thirst for the Lord increase our ability to receive more from Him.

One mother carried a four-year-old child named Carlos in her arms. She testified that her son was born missing a testicle, but when I declared the wave of creative miracles, her son started crying. She checked him, and to her great joy she found that the missing organ was now in place. With tears in her eyes, the mother shared that before, all she could feel was an empty sac, but now her son has both testicles. God created the missing organ in little Carlos!

Hunger for more of God caused William, a fifty-one-year-old man, to receive his miracle as well. He was born with a rolled ear, meaning that where the ear opening would normally be, it was closed with flesh. William shared that this had caused him to be deaf in that ear since birth. However, he testified that God created an eardrum because, even though the ear is still closed, he can now hear perfectly. "My doctors told me my eardrum had never formed, but now I hear from that ear!"

CAP attracts leaders from across the world who are hungry and thirsty for what only God can offer. This past year, angelic activity and creative miracles started manifesting as a result of the people's hunger and thirst for God. In the midst of that atmosphere, Pastor Zennie, from

Georgia, USA, shared that fifteen years previously, the left side of her thyroid had been removed. However, she testified that when I declared that the Lord was sending angels with new body parts for those who were in need of a creative miracle, she saw the hands of an angel coming to her. "I simply closed my eyes and raised my hands to the sky, and I felt a deep burning in my throat. When I opened my eyes, I knew something had happened and that I had received the organ I needed. When I went to a doctor to get a checkup, the tests showed my thyroid was whole and healthy. To God be the glory!"

Hunger and thirst for God are signs of humility.

The arena where we held the CAP conference was filled with additional signs and angelic activity. Many people had oil, gold dust, and other signs of the Spirit manifest on their hands or clothing. Some members of the audience had visions of angels, while others were spiritually transported, similar to what happened to the apostle Philip in the New Testament. (See Acts 8:39–40.) Yasser, a member of our local church, shares that he was in deep worship with four other people when they entered a dimension where they were as light as feathers. He said, "It was something I had never felt in my life or in my relationship with God. Suddenly our group realized we were all at the end of our section, and we were surprised to see that our seats were on the other side of us. We looked at one another, knowing we had been teleported by God. He showed us a sign of the end times!"

Rosa, another woman from our church, testified that she saw four angels before her. One of them asked her, "What do you want me to do for you?" She answered, "I want my scholarship to be able to study and my immigration documents to be approved." Two days after the conference, she received confirmation that her Social Security card was in the mail. She testifies, "Now I am a legal resident of this country!"

Are you satisfied with the revivals of the past? Are you full of traditional Christianity, where nothing supernatural happens and where there are no miracles because although God is spoken of, His power is never shown? Do you want revival in your life, in your family, and in your church? Are you desperate for the Lord to use you in miracles, healings, and deliverances? Are you willing to pay the price, to withstand criticism from other people, to move in the power of God, to love the Holy Spirit, and to manifest the supernatural? If you want more of God, His Word promises, "Blessed are you who hunger now, for you shall be filled" (Luke 6:21).

3. DENY YOURSELF

To be baptized and filled with the Holy Spirit requires death, and that death is saying no to "self." Denying yourself means renouncing your ambitions, opinions, comfort, and the pleasures of the flesh to seek the things of God. For some believers, this means renouncing the mentality that speaking in tongues was a gift only in the past. As we have seen, Jesus' baptism was an act of renouncing. To Him, the Jordan represented death to self, surrendering His will to do the will of the Father. There are no shortcuts to access the power of God because it comes only when we say no to our own desires. The mind-set of the world is to do things in our own strength, but the way of God is to allow Him to use us as extensions of His power.

One of leadership's greatest traps is thinking we have arrived, that we have it all, just because we have achieved a little success.

You will be anointed in proportion to how much you have died to yourself and surrendered to the Holy Spirit. When you die to the things of the world, you will no longer be prey to temptation. You will not love fleeting pleasures or be attracted to the enemy's offers of vain satisfaction. Only when you are in this state will the Holy Spirit fill you.

Know the true fullness of the Spirit, and be so filled with Him that there is no room for anything else.

> **Christ had anointing without limit because He completely surrendered to God.**

BE FILLED DIRECTLY BY THE HOLY SPIRIT

There is no excuse for not being baptized with the Holy Spirit or filled with Him. In the times in which we now live, going to church is not enough. Wicked thoughts and life's cares and worries may disappear momentarily when you are under the covering, under the presence of the almighty God, during a church service. However, when you leave church and go back to your home, you may feel empty again. This means you depend on an exterior atmosphere, instead of being filled from within by the Spirit of God. You cannot expect to live continually in church, surrounded by an atmosphere created by God and in the midst of your brothers and sisters in the faith; you need to be filled directly by the Holy Spirit. This is the only way you will fill the void in your spirit and start walking in the power of God, healing the sick and casting out demons. This is the time for you to say, "Lord, I want something different. I refuse to accept the same Christianity; I don't want to go back to it, and I don't want to be limited. Baptize me and fill me with Your Holy Spirit."

ACTIVATION

Do you struggle with wicked thoughts, bad habits, and constant worrying? Take them captive to the obedience of Jesus and be filled with the Holy Spirit. As we have noted, we need to receive directly from the Spirit so that we can truly be filled. Let your hunger and thirst grow for health, peace, and power, and let those needs be met by the Holy Spirit. Renounce everything the world offers and your flesh demands. Make room for God to be the One who satisfies you with His love, power, and grace. Allow Him to make you supernatural, to enable you to overcome the world, and to turn you into an agent of change for others.

I invite you to pray the following:

Heavenly Father, I come before Your presence as a born-again believer who has received Jesus as Lord and Savior. I thank You for the experience of salvation, but I know You have more for me. You want me to be baptized and filled with Your Holy Spirit, with the evidence of speaking in other tongues. Lord, forgive me if I have believed in doctrines that quench Your gifts, tongues, miracles, and supernatural power; forgive me for thinking these were things of the past and ended in the age of the apostles. Holy Spirit, forgive me! Heavenly Father, I ask that You lead me to the truth. Give me hunger and thirst for You, and use me to demonstrate Your power. Baptize me and fill me as promised in Your Word. I ask that Your Spirit dwell in me all the days of my life. Submerge me in Your power and miracles. I receive the fullness of the Holy Spirit now, in the name of Jesus.

The initial evidence that you have been filled and baptized with the Holy Spirit is tongues. Start now to speak in other tongues. Remember that the Holy Spirit will not *make* you speak in tongues; He gives them to you, but you have to *say* them. Begin to worship God in your spiritual language, and as you do, the Holy Spirit will start to fill you up and give you more. Keep speaking in tongues…this means you have already been baptized with the Holy Spirit. At the very moment you are baptized, you are also authorized to exercise power and authority, to demonstrate the power and finished work of Christ on the cross. Wherever you go, I commission you to heal the sick, cast out demons, free the captives, and raise the dead.

The following is a prayer for every believer who has been baptized in the Holy Spirit but wants a fresh encounter. Pray with me:

> Heavenly Father, I have been fighting the enemy, sowing, praying for the sick, and preaching the Word, but it has been a long time since I was filled by Your Spirit. I have been leaking in my spirit, and today I need You to fill me again. I ask in the name of Jesus for a fresh outpouring, because I desperately need to be filled with the Holy Spirit.

Right now, I pray that the Holy Spirit will invade you with a fresh fullness, so that you will go out again to preach the Word, win souls, and heal the sick. And so that you will return to war against the enemy, the flesh, and temptations, and overcome all opposition. Now, be filled with the Holy Spirit, from the crown of your head to the soles of your feet. Be filled in your mind, in your body, and in your spirit, in the name of Jesus! Amen!

7

HOW TO BE LED BY
THE HOLY SPIRIT

When believers are baptized and filled with the Holy Spirit, the next step in their walk with God is to discern His guidance, follow His direction, and train their spiritual gifts. When the Spirit of God has priority in our lives, He protects us from falling into the traps, temptations, attacks, and lies of the enemy. The Holy Spirit reveals the will of the Father for each moment of our lives and leads us to manifest His power against all odds. He is the One who gives us a precise answer for every ministry situation, such as letting us know when someone needs a miracle, when someone needs to forgive another person in order to be freed from pain or sickness, or when someone is being attacked by an evil spirit, so we can deliver them.

In this chapter, I will describe how the guidance of the Holy Spirit works, show you practical ways to follow His direction, and activate you to make decisions under His presence.

UNDERSTANDING THE DIRECTION AND GUIDANCE OF THE HOLY SPIRIT

The journey of our spiritual life begins with a knowledge of our destiny, though this is not easy to discern. Some people have no clue about what their purpose in life is. Others know where they are headed, but may not know how to get there. Many people go in search of something that is outside the will of God because they lack the guidance of the Holy Spirit.

Can you tell when you are being led by God? Can you perceive His guidance? If we lack the Holy Spirit's direction, we will fail in our walk with God. The Holy Spirit will always lead us toward the destiny God has planned for our life. Without Him, we will never really know Jesus and His finished work on the cross or enter our glorious destiny with Him.

No matter how much progress we make in a certain direction, we will not discover our destiny by following that course if the will of God is for us to go in a different direction. If we don't know our purpose, we will make mistakes at every crossroad on the path. As a result, we will get sidetracked and become disappointed and discouraged. That is why it is so important for us to learn to recognize the guidance and direction of the Spirit of God. Any believer who accepts being led by Him will come to know and understand the purpose for which they were called.

One of the questions I am frequently asked when I travel around the world is, "How can I be led by the Holy Spirit?" People see how my life and ministry are led by the Spirit of God, and the way He moves throughout our services to heal, deliver, and give words of wisdom to His sons and daughters. I seek the guidance of the Spirit in the decisions I make for my family, for the ministry, and for everything God tells us to do. It humbles my heart when people ask me how they can live in the same way, and I gladly reveal to them the principles I apply, because it is my passion for every believer to manifest the kingdom of God and its power. The following principles will help you to discern the guidance of the Holy Spirit.

1. THE HOLY SPIRIT LEADS AND DIRECTS, BUT HE DOES NOT CONTROL

True authority does not control, but rather leads and directs. When we are led, we voluntarily walk under the authority of another; in this case, under the authority of Jesus through the Holy Spirit. In contrast, when you are controlled by something or someone, you are *obligated* to do things by force, whether or not you want to. That is how demons operate. They clash with an individual's will until the person submits to them. The Holy Spirit never forces people. Instead, He works by giving us revelation, which helps us to willingly yield to Him so that He may work in us and through us.

2. THE HOLY SPIRIT GUIDES US PERSONALLY, WHILE HIS PRINCIPLES ARE UNIVERSAL

To live according to God's principles is to live by what He has said. The principles of God will work for anyone, whether they are a believer or not, because the principles are universal. However, living by the guidance of the Holy Spirit is only for the children of God because it involves what He is saying and doing in the now. As believers, we must trust in the personal guidance of the Holy Spirit. Following His guidance accelerates spiritual breakthroughs in every stagnant area of our lives, gives direction for reaching our destiny, and enables us to complete our purpose.

To better understand the difference between the principles of God and the guidance of God, we can say that the principles of God are like a map that directs us through the different roads to reach a destination, but we have to choose the path we want to take, even when we don't know what obstacles will present themselves along the way. However, the guidance of the Holy Spirit is much like a GPS system that leads us to the exact location we seek. The Spirit speaks to us and shows us the road step-by-step; He tells us where there is "traffic" and other obstacles along the route before we encounter them, so we can avoid them or be prepared to address them. If we find ourselves in a desert, trying to find our way, or if we get into other trouble, the voice of the Holy Spirit asks, "Can I help you?" If we answer "Yes," He will take us by the hand and pull us out of danger.

Nonetheless, once we feel safe, it often happens that we put aside the Holy Spirit's guidance and try to rely on our own sense of direction. If we do that, and continue to repeat this behavior, the Holy Spirit will leave us because we indicate we do not need Him, believing that we can do things in our own strength or by the law. If this is the case with you, you have the opportunity today to choose: either be led by principles alone, or allow yourself to be led by the person of the Holy Spirit. He is the wise Counselor who knows your destiny and what is and is not best for you; He is the One who leads you to God's will and blessings and who will manifest His plan for your life. Choose today to be led by the Holy Spirit!

3. THE HOLY SPIRIT SHOWS US THE WAYS OF GOD

"He made known His ways to Moses, His acts to the children of Israel" (Psalm 103:7). Knowing the *ways* of the Lord is different from knowing His *works*. The ways of God include the desires and motivations of His heart and the manner in which He does things. The works of God are His supernatural and visible acts. The Bible tells us that the children of Israel knew the works of God but remained ignorant of His ways for forty years. They did not treasure His Word; on the contrary, they rejected it. Many times, they went against what Moses told them even though he was the leader appointed by God.

Similarly, when believers reject the Word and the guidance of the Holy Spirit, they remain ignorant of God's ways. As a result, they will not see the promises of God fulfilled in their lives. Every generation in which the Spirit of God dwells is one that recognizes His ways. Let us pray for this to happen with our generation.

> There are two means by which we can know the ways of God: by His Word and by the guidance of the Holy Spirit.

4. THE HOLY SPIRIT LEADS US FROM THE INSIDE, NOT THE OUTSIDE

"And the Lord *went before them by day in a pillar of cloud to lead the way, and by night in a pillar of fire to give them light, so as to go by day and night"* (Exodus 13:21). In the Old Testament, God led Israel with His visible glory, such as the pillar of cloud and pillar of fire. Yet ever since Jesus' victory on the cross and resurrection, the Holy Spirit has lived inside God's people and guided them from within. *"If the Spirit of Him who raised Jesus from the dead dwells in you, He who raised Christ from the dead will also give life to your mortal bodies through His Spirit who dwells in you"* (Romans 8:11).

Many people are looking for something visible to guide them so they can believe and follow God. They want something their eyes can see and their minds can understand, but the Holy Spirit directs us internally in various ways. Since the Spirit lives within us, we must learn to recognize His voice and other communications. His voice does not come from above or below; it comes from inside us. Our need to continually hear His voice is another reason why we must always be filled with the Spirit.

5. THE HOLY SPIRIT GUIDES US FROM A REALM OF INNOCENCE

By *innocence*, I mean we must recognize that we are completely ignorant about certain situations, and that true knowledge comes from the Holy Spirit. The Word says, *"The Spirit also helps in our weaknesses. For we do not know what we should pray for as we ought, but the Spirit Himself makes intercession for us with groanings which cannot be uttered"* (Romans 8:26). Every time I ask the Spirit to lead me, it is because I do not know what is going on in my life or because I want to know about the root of something that is causing a problem. I do it in order to help people or to manifest God's power. Allow me to explain this with a few examples.

On a certain occasion, I was invited by two of my spiritual children, Apostle Jorge Ledesma and his wife, Prophet Alicia, to preach at a soccer stadium in Argentina. The invitation was for the purpose of ministering about finances and leading the people to financially support the building of their new church. I thought all I would do would be to pray for financial miracles.

In that soccer stadium, where roughly twenty-seven thousand people had come together, the atmosphere was ready for financial miracles; however, in the middle of the service, the Holy Spirit suddenly led me to minister creative miracles. In my mind, this made little sense, and I did not know how to make the transition, but He guided me. I was able to release the power of God, and many people were healed that day.

The Spirit of God led me to pray this: "Father, in the name of Jesus, I bind every spirit from hell and I take authority over the spirits of sickness that attack your people. I send your angels now and give them an order. Angels: place new organs in the bodies of those who are missing them. New eardrums, cartilage, hips, kidneys, skin, thyroids, vertebrae, teeth, bones, knees, wombs, and more: all are created by the hand of God!" All I needed to do was make that decree. No one touched the people or went to lay hands on them. However, seventy creative miracles were documented in a span of fifteen minutes.

One of the testimonies that moved me the most was that of a young man named Lucas, who came to the meeting missing half the bones of his cranium. He shared that when he was a teenager, he had been held up at gunpoint in his neighborhood. During the struggle, he was struck in the head and left unconscious. He was taken to the hospital and remained in a coma for five days due to the damage to his skull and brain. The doctors had to remove part of the parietal lobe and occipital bone, and this essentially left him with a hole in his head, causing severe headaches and sensitivity to sunlight.

The Holy Spirit had spoken to Lucas previously, telling him that his creative miracle would come soon. When he was told I would be in Argentina for a conference, he saw it as a confirmation from God and attended the meeting. He testified that when I prayed for creative miracles, he felt a strong fire, a type of incision in his head, and unbearable pressure. When he went to the altar to testify what he was feeling, a doctor checked him and saw that the bone he had been missing just a few minutes before was now there! God had created bone where there wasn't any! And the constant migraine headaches and pressure in his head were gone. Lucas says that it has been months since he received his miracle, but he feels no pain and can be in the sunlight without any problems.

The guidance of the Spirit is for those who humble themselves and ask from a realm of innocence.

In a previous trip I had made to Argentina, one of the most powerful miracles I had seen involved a woman named Alejandra, who'd had a breast removed because of cancer, but God had created a new one for her. Now, in this latest visit, Alejandra received another creative miracle. This is her testimony:

"Three years after my breast grew back, my doctor detected that the cancer had resurfaced and had metastasized to my spine. The disease was eating away at two of my vertebrae, so I went into surgery and had them removed, causing me to remain bound to a wheelchair from that day. As a result, a hole formed in my back that caused me unbearable pain, and I had to take as many as ten morphine pills a day. However, I remained firm in believing that the same God who had saved me before would do so again. Thus, when I heard that Apostle Maldonado was returning to Argentina, I prayed for the Lord to do another creative miracle in me, and that is just what happened. The moment the Apostle started declaring creative miracles, I felt heat in my back. I cried out with joy because I could physically feel my back being healed. When I got to the altar to share my testimony, the doctors there could feel that the two vertebrae had regrown. The Lord created new bones in my body! Today I lead a healthy life, and I feel as though I have been born again."

Every believer has the potential of being led by the Holy Spirit, just as Jesus was.

6. THE HOLY SPIRIT'S GUIDANCE IS SUPERNATURAL

When we allow the Holy Spirit to lead us, His supernatural power manifests in our lives. If this is not happening, it means we are not allowing ourselves to be led by Him. Personally, every time I follow His direction, it is manifested by signs, miracles, supernatural grace, and provision. For example, there have been occasions when I have been ministering at church and suddenly the Holy Spirit has led me to pray for specific people, and they have been healed before my eyes.

WAYS IN WHICH THE HOLY SPIRIT LEADS US

Let us now turn to specific ways in which the Spirit leads us.

THROUGH OUR INTUITION

Intuition is the ability to understand something instantly, without the need for conscious reasoning. Intuition is not the same thing as instinct. All of us have a degree of instinct, which is defined as "a natural or inherent aptitude, impulse, or capacity." But whereas instinct is a physical quality—even animals have a form of it—intuition is spiritual; it is part of our renewed spirit when we are born again.

Intuition is not something we study to learn but rather something we know inside because the Spirit reveals it to us. If we tried to understand our intuition through reason, it would make no scientific or common sense to us, because it requires the guidance of the Holy Spirit. Let us consider this reality based on a testimony from one of my spiritual daughters, Apostle Patty Valenzuela, from Los Angeles, California, who shared with me the following.

"I am sincerely grateful for the teachings of my spiritual father, Apostle Guillermo Maldonado, and how he instructs me to follow the guidance of the Holy Spirit. Sometimes I have the privilege of speaking with him on the telephone before I preach. Although we are two thousand miles apart, the Holy Spirit has revealed specific situations to him that members of my congregation were experiencing.

"I remember one time he told me, 'Daughter, there is a couple whose son is in a coma in the hospital; also, there is a young girl suffering from depression, and a man with a herniated disc that is causing him severe pain.' Without thinking twice, I obeyed the words of knowledge he received by releasing them in that order during the service. And those people were all there! The couple had a newborn baby who was still in the hospital and in a coma. After we prayed, God worked the miracle; the doctors took the baby off the artificial breathing machines he had been connected to because he no longer needed them. The young girl whom the Apostle saw in a vision was planning to commit suicide later that night; the Lord delivered her from depression during the same service. The last one was a truck driver who went to the service with terrible back pains because of a herniated disk; God healed him, and now he is pain-free!"

From all of this, I have learned that if we allow ourselves to be led by God and are obedient to Him, then the Holy Spirit will move with power, and Jesus will be glorified! I remember that while I prayed with Apostle Patty, I had felt an intuition that those three cases would be present during that service. It was a sudden feeling, and as I received it, I released it. Perhaps it made no sense at the time, but I bypassed my reason and followed the intuition of the Spirit.

Every believer can receive the Holy Spirit's intuition because He lives inside of us and reveals to us our environment. He leads us where we need to go, frequently to a reality we don't know anything about, but where He produces supernatural manifestations. In this new place, there are miracles, grace, and power that the Lord wants to release through us; to manifest them, He deposits intuition into our spirits. What should we do when we receive it? Release it! If we try to reason out what we are feeling, there will be no manifestation because the power is connected to the action, not the logic. We must act in faith, believing in the intuition of the Spirit.

The following illustration of this truth happened when I went to minister in Norway, a completely secular country. On that occasion, I asked the Holy Spirit what He wanted me to teach and minister. Instantly, intuition came into my spirit, and I knew I had to minister deliverance. I had been told by countless people that Norway was not used to witnessing the supernatural, that it was very intellectual, and that when Norwegians witnessed the manifestation of demons during deliverance, they would get scared, but I followed the instructions of the Spirit. I ministered miracles and deliverance, and because of this the people met a God of power. Of all the miracles that occurred, these two testimonies impressed me the most:

"My name is Marivic, and I live in Oslo, Norway. I went to Apostle Maldonado's conference at the Telenor Arena with hope that the Lord would do great things, and I was not disappointed. I needed to be delivered from the bondage of religion, depression, doubt, confusion, failure, demonic oppression, the fear of death, and the spirit of death. I truly believed that the Lord would heal me, but the supernatural is not normal here in Norway, and most people don't believe in deliverance. This did not stop me. Apostle Maldonado taught that the blood of Jesus has power, and he demonstrated that fact. His prayer was, 'Father, let Your kingdom come, let Your will be done and touch these people, and I declare they are free, now!' I fell without realizing it, and I could hear myself screaming, rolling on the ground, and completely losing control of myself. I was shouting from the bottom of my stomach and jumping all over the place. I wanted to speak the name of Jesus, but I couldn't; every time I tried, my tongue would freeze up. Finally, I was able to shout His name, and I went home knowing I had been delivered. When I went to sleep, the enemy tried to attack me again, but this time I felt the love of God flooding through me. When I woke up, I felt clean, and the tormenting thoughts that I had always struggled with had been replaced with His peace. From here in Norway, I experienced the delivering power of God!"

The second testimony is from Larisa, a woman born in Cameroon, who testified about how God healed her as she watched the conference online, miles away from the location.

"For the last month, I had been suffering from pain in my lungs. One day I woke up scared because I was coughing blood, and the situation worsened when I started having dreams about my death. I went to the hospital to get my lungs checked because they felt full of liquid and I could barely breathe. Though I went through many tests to determine if I had cancer, the doctors could not find the source, and the bleeding continued. Back at home, while I watched the conference, I listened to Apostle Maldonado, and I cried to the Lord for Him to heal me. Suddenly, I saw the Apostle turn to the screen and say, 'There is a woman watching who needs new lungs.' I had never believed much in TV preachers, but at that moment I fell on my knees and cried out, 'My Lord, I need You to heal me and deliver me.' Immediately, I felt strong heat on my chest and the power of the Holy Spirit. A few minutes later, I realized I could breathe without any problems, the pain in my chest had disappeared, and I no longer coughed blood. The power of God completely amazed me! It was already 10:00 p.m., but nothing could stop me from dropping off my children with their father, purchasing a train ticket to Oslo, and going to the conference so I could testify that God had healed me!"

THROUGH OUR INNER WITNESS, OR BY AN IMPRESSION

The inner witness is an impression from the Spirit that is distinct from intuition. We perceive something about a situation that has not yet happened but that we spiritually see the evidence of in the now. Years might pass before something takes place, but we can already envision it in our mind's eye.

The impressions of the Spirit are part of the nature of the prophetic. Romans 8:16 tells us that *"the Spirit Himself bears witness with our spirit that we are children of God."* It is important for us to recognize that the Spirit wants to bear witness with our spirit, and not to let our minds and hearts be contaminated by other things that might influence our spirit. When I go to minister at a service, I need to prepare myself in prayer and fasting, but I also need to keep my spirit clean of all sin and distractions, including evil thoughts, grudges, wicked desires, and bad impressions.

I almost never speak to others before I preach, because if I do, I run the risk of having a second impression enter my spirit and interrupt the ministration of the Word of God. If someone tells me a problem, that can burden me. Any other kind of information that does not come from the Spirit can mix with the thoughts I have received from God and become a stumbling block when I try to release the provision of God with purity over His people.

In order to receive the impressions of the Spirit, you do not need to be taught, but you must be activated and trained. Then the Spirit of God will begin to bring these impressions to your heart repeatedly. When you receive an inner witness from God, you have a clear confidence about it in your spirit, but if you do not obey it right away, the impression becomes weaker, and you become easily distracted from it. (The exception is if the inner witness is clearly for the future.) An impression does not leave your mind unless you reject it, but if you do, it will diminish until it disappears. This is why it is so important that we receive the Holy Spirit's impressions and obey Him as soon as He speaks to us.

The first sign that you are not interested in the things of the Holy Spirit is that you do not pay attention to these impressions, and they mean nothing to you. However, when you have the witness of the Spirit, you know what they mean, and they manifest as a strong conviction inside you.

The first impression is normally the one of the Spirit.

For example, in light of what I have just described, I can confirm, for several reasons, that I was completely led by the Holy Spirit to make a ministry trip to Pakistan. Many people do not go to Pakistan because it is a country where there is extreme terrorism. Someone must really receive a strong impression from the Spirit to know that they are walking in the will of God and His protection when they go there. When I was invited to Pakistan by my spiritual son, Apostle Ankwar, I prayed to the Lord and felt the guidance of the Holy Spirit. I asked Him what His purpose was for leading me to that country, and He told me He wanted me to preach about the cross there.

Once I arrived, I found myself before 1.2 million people. I preached about the finished work of Christ on the cross, and thousands upon thousands were saved and healed because I followed the impression of the Holy Spirit. All the people were blessed because I let Him lead me. Likewise, in every preaching and teaching opportunity, as well as in every personal decision I make, I always ask the Holy Spirit to lead me; and many times, His voice comes to me as an intuition or as an inner witness or impression, such as those I have just described.

The impressions of the Spirit lead us to make decisions in life.

BY THE WORD OF GOD

The genuine guidance of the Spirit is always clear; there is no confusion, contradiction, or doubt in it. The psalmist said, *"Your word is a lamp to my feet and a light to my path"* (Psalm 119:105). God's Word is our lamp and our light. As a lamp, the Word leads us to make the right choices and to position ourselves to receive the blessings of God. Many times the Lord has led me to make a decision by reminding me of a Bible verse confirming that what I am feeling is a true intuition or impression because it doesn't contradict the Bible but instead aligns with it.

BY AN INNER VOICE

Similarly, the inner voice of the Spirit always speaks according to God's nature and character; it never contradicts them. This inner voice is the intimate one we hear in our spirit, directing us what to do. We learn to hear it by walking with God in a permanent relationship with Him. Romans 8:14 says that those who *"are led by the Spirit of God, these are sons of God."*

Some time ago, I was praying at home when the Lord spoke to my heart, telling me to go to Mexico. I started to make all the travel arrangements to go there with my Missions team, and I kept praying for the Lord to reveal to me His will for this trip. Finally the Holy Spirit spoke to me and said, "I want you to go to Mexico and declare open heavens over that nation." It was the first time I had received this type of commission, and I did not know how I would carry it out, but He instructed me to make this decree of "open heavens" during the second night of the services.

Because the Lord showed me that He would open the heavens over Mexico, that is what I declared. Once I had done what He revealed to me through the inner voice, then healings and deliverances started to happen. These miracles were similar to ones I had already seen many times before, so I asked the Lord what the difference was between them and "open heavens," and He replied that I would see the difference the next day. In the last sessions, while we worshipped the Holy Spirit, the presence of God fell, and the sick started to be healed on their own. We saw outstanding miracles, many of them happening all at once, without anyone laying hands on people. The following is a recap of the most impactful testimonies.

> **Those who don't know how to hear the Word, or don't bother to learn how to do so, are not worthy to hear Him.**

Maricela had been suffering from allergic rhinitis for twelve years. It was a generational curse, and her grandmother, her mother, herself, and her son had been diagnosed with the same disease. She could not breathe well, her sense of smell was nearly gone, and she could not even run because she would get exhausted quickly. Maricela testified that as soon as I declared open heavens over Mexico, she felt something hot going down her forehead, and immediately her nose was cleared; she could even smell the popcorn in the stadium. Now she can run, and she's completely healed!

Laura Cecilia suffered from schizophrenia. In addition, she was born with maxillofacial dysplasia, a hollow in the upper jaw that deformed her head and face, because of a generational curse. Her paternal grandparents and her father had had the same illness. Now, not only she but also her brothers suffered from the condition. Before the miracles began, that hollow part of her skull was smooth and felt soft, but when her miracle occurred, she suddenly felt an intense heat starting from behind her head and moving to the front. When the doctor at the altar checked her, he could feel the missing bone forming, and the skull beginning to harden. Laura Cecilia claims that God freed her from schizophrenia in the midst of worship and also created the bone that was missing in her head.

Alexis had suffered a stroke two years earlier, leading to a clot forming in his brain stem. Because of this, he arrived at the Mexico Supernatural Encounter unable to walk by himself, and feeling oppression in his head and constant dizziness. He could not work because of his disability, and being a young man, he did not want to continue to live like this. Alexis says that when I declared creative miracles under open heavens, he raised his hands and for several minutes felt fire and lightning all over his body. He immediately released the walking cane he had depended on. Now he could not only walk, but also run. God had healed him, and the stroke was a thing of the past!

Alejandra had been diagnosed with redundant spastic colon, which is a condition in the digestive tract, specifically in the large intestine. When she learned that I was coming to Mexico, she decided to attend the Supernatural Encounter, knowing she would receive her miracle. Alejandra says that on that Friday when I asked the people to put their hands wherever they had any pain or illness, she put her hand over her stomach area and asked God to heal her. Suddenly she felt very hot, and it seemed as if something were coming off her body. Alejandra testifies that she has not needed to take any more medication. "I have not had any more pain! Before I could not eat fats, because afterward I had to take up to twenty-four pills a day. Now, the Lord healed me and gave me a new stomach!"

If God can speak to me clearly and use me so strongly, He can do the same for you. All you need to do is learn how to hear His voice and follow it. As you learn to hear, I urge you to follow His voice, impressions, and intuition, because you have the potential to be used by God.

> **The inner witness of the Holy Spirit will lead to you to act and walk in the supernatural, and to have glorious encounters with Him.**

PREPARING TO BE LED BY THE HOLY SPIRIT

God never intended for us to walk aimlessly, trying to please Him without guidance or direction. Instead, He sent us the Holy Spirit and equipped us with the ability to hear, feel, intuit, and discern His atmosphere. You too can be guided by the Holy Spirit, just as the early Christians were, by doing the following.

GIVE YOURSELF TO A LIFE OF CONSTANT PRAYER

The first key to being led by the Spirit of God is living a life of constant prayer and communion with God, as Jesus did; this is the formula for remaining in a supernatural state where our every step is aligned with God's plans and will. Prayer is communication with the Father, through which we receive His guidance and direction. And it is the Holy Spirit who enables us to express our deepest needs and requests to the Father. *"Likewise the Spirit also helps in our weaknesses. For we do not know what we should pray for as we ought, but the Spirit Himself makes intercession for us with groanings which cannot be uttered"* (Romans 8:26).

YIELD AND SURRENDER TO THE SPIRIT

Yielding to the Spirit means obedience and surrender, trading the natural of man for the supernatural of God. It is an act that comes from our own will. Again, the Holy Spirit does not make us do things by force, but He does instruct us. In the desert, when Moses approached the burning bush, God told him, *"Do not draw near this place. Take your sandals off your feet, for the place where you stand is holy ground"* (Exodus 3:5). We must yield to God's instructions and surrender our unbelief, doubts, weaknesses, selfish desires, emotions, thoughts, and fears to the Holy Spirit. We must die to ourselves—to the flesh and to our natural senses—so He may lead us to walk in the supernatural.

Jesus' anointing was without limits because He surrendered everything He had; He didn't hold anything back. He was completely led by the Spirit because He did not focus on Himself but on what the Spirit told Him to say and do. The same outlook is available to us. If we want to operate under the guidance and anointing of the Holy Spirit without limits, then we must surrender everything, without limits. I am frequently told, "Apostle, I want to increase the anointing and guidance of the Spirit in my life. What do I do?" My answer is always, "You must deny yourself and yield all of yourself to the Spirit of God." This is the only way His anointing will increase in us, so that we can be used by Him to minister under open heavens, with all of the power of God. When there is less of us, there is more of Him—but the opposite is true as well.

The Christian life does not consist of struggling but of yielding. It is not an effort but a choice that comes from our union with the Holy Spirit.

Every time we die to our rights, Jesus Christ gives us His rights, the same ones He won on the cross of Calvary. This is the law of exchange that I mentioned in a previous chapter. In this exchange, the Lord tells us, "I am going to give you more power, but I want you to surrender your fears, doubts, and unbelief. I am going to give you more wisdom, but I want you to surrender your ambitions and personal agenda to Me." To yield and surrender to the Spirit is to let God be God, in us and through us. We can know that no exchange has taken place if there is no increase in anointing, so we must examine our hearts to see to what extent we have yielded to God.

The guidance of the Holy Spirit in our lives increases in accordance with the measure that we surrender to Him. *"He must increase, but I must decrease"* (John 3:30). The more we yield to God, the more the life of Christ will dwell in us. All of us have something to surrender to Him; it may be riches, wicked thoughts, discouragement, immaturity, inconsistency, unforgiveness, impure relationships, ambition, or other things. We must make a commitment to give over to God whatever we are holding on to. We cannot allow anything in our lives to become an idol or to get in the way of the Holy Spirit's work in us or through us.

Thus, we will have the power of the Holy Spirit in the same amount or measure that we yield ourselves to God. Do you have 30 percent of Christ? That 30 percent is what you have surrendered to Him. If you give Him 100 percent, you will receive 100 percent in return. That is why the apostle Paul told the Galatians, *"I have been crucified with Christ; it is no longer I who live, but Christ lives in me; and the life which I now live in the flesh I live by faith in the Son of God, who loved me and gave Himself for me"* (Galatians 2:20).

WALK IN THE SPIRIT, AND NOT THE FLESH

During the course of our lives, we will always face conflicts between our spirit and our flesh because *"the spirit indeed is willing, but the flesh is weak"* (Matthew 26:41). As human beings, we have three dimensions— spirit, soul, and body. A child of God who is led and influenced by the

Holy Spirit operates from the first dimension, which is that of the spirit. Our spiritual man is formed when we are born again and is developed by obedience to the Word and being led by the Holy Spirit; this is the perfect balance in the spiritual realm. The spiritual man wants more of God and less of himself, therefore, he longs for the guidance of the Holy Spirit.

Those who live in the flesh operate in the second dimension of their humanity—the soul, which is the place where perversions are born. That is why they are selfish, self-absorbed, ambitious, and undisciplined, having uncontrollable appetites. They want more of themselves and less of God.

Living according to the desires of our flesh is the same as being led by our sinful nature. Accordingly, the proof that someone is living in the flesh is that their actions and decisions are not led by the Holy Spirit. For example, if their emotions are out of control, then they are not walking under the influence of the Spirit. Moreover, walking in the flesh opens the door to temptation; it is one way of saying "Yes" to the offers of the enemy. When we are walking in that condition, the Holy Spirit cannot guide us.

According to the Bible, the "flesh" is anything that lacks the influence of the Holy Spirit.

We cannot walk with the Spirit of God if we don't crucify our flesh daily. Any day I fail to crucify my flesh, I can make the worst mistakes. Thus, at the end of each day, I can look back upon the choices I have made and see whether I was led by my flesh or by my spirit, if I was influenced by the old nature or by the Spirit of God.

To be led by the Holy Spirit is to walk under His influence. That means we no longer do things according to the desires of our flesh. The Word of God teaches us to renew our minds so that we can think as Jesus does and allow ourselves to be led by the Spirit. (See Romans 12:2.) *"For God has not given us a spirit of fear, but of power and of love and of a sound mind"* (2 Timothy 1:7).

> **The way to avoid being led by the flesh is to be filled with the Spirit of God so that we can be led by Him in all things.**

If you are fighting with matters of the flesh, go to the cross. That is the place where Jesus died, where He paid the price for our redemption and released His power upon us to overcome the flesh. Crucifying the flesh is part of our priesthood, of presenting ourselves as a living sacrifice before God and leaving our old nature at the altar. (See Romans 12:1.) This new priesthood comes in the form of spiritual offerings like praying, fasting, giving, and worshipping. When we are in that state of sacrifice, the Holy Spirit can speak to our inner being, lead us to all truth and to the will of God, and release His power over us. We must sacrifice our old man, or old nature, in order for our new spiritual man to live. *"But the natural man does not receive the things of the Spirit of God, for they are foolishness to him; nor can he know them, because they are spiritually discerned"* (1 Corinthians 2:14).

For many people, there is nothing more real than their logic and their fleshly nature. They consider their problems, impossibilities, and fears to be more substantial than the Holy Spirit. However, the moment you stop living in the flesh and live in the Spirit, the Spirit of God becomes more real to you, and you can discern His guidance and direction. He becomes more important than the desires of your flesh. When you are led by the Spirit, you lead a holy life, and even your natural senses are sanctified.

Jesus Christ is the Person I most admire, because as a man He showed us that we can live in victory if we totally yield to God and walk in the Spirit. We see a strong illustration of this in Jesus' wilderness temptation. *"Then Jesus was led up by the Spirit into the wilderness to be tempted by the devil"* (Matthew 4:1). The Spirit of God directed Jesus to the desert so He could follow the steps that would lead Him to the fulfillment of His purpose. Note that although Jesus was tempted by the enemy, He allowed Himself to be led by the Spirit.

Through Jesus' example, the Father showed mankind how to overcome the enemy's temptation. Recall that when Jesus came to earth, He left His divine attributes behind in heaven. Philippians 2:7 says that He *"gave up His divine privileges"* (NLT). He became man so He could model for us a life guided by the Spirit. He never fell into sin, and He reached the glorious destiny that the Father had prepared for Him.

Jesus Christ showed us how to defeat the enemy, overcome temptation, and please the Father in all things.

I choose to believe it was not a coincidence that Jesus faced the devil in the desert. The enemy saw an opportunity to deceive the Son of God in a similar way that he had with Adam and Eve; but he was surprised when Jesus did not yield to any of his temptations. The flesh was not Jesus' reality, because He was so completely filled with the Spirit of God. Similarly, until the Holy Spirit becomes more real to you than the flesh and the natural realm, you will never overcome temptation successfully. Are fame, sex, money, pride, or food more real to you than the Holy Spirit? If so, then you will always yield to whatever trap the enemy places in front of you. In his own strength, a natural human being cannot overcome the devil. Without the Holy Spirit, you cannot even fight the enemy, much less defeat him.

The temptations you cannot overcome tell you how much of the life of God you are still missing, and the temptations you overcome reveal how much of the Holy Spirit's anointing you carry. Remember that the Lord gives us His Spirit so we can overcome temptation just as Jesus did. This means that every believer has the potential, the ability, to be led by the Spirit of God, because He lives inside of us and because Jesus has shown us how to listen to His voice.

BE LED BY THE HOLY SPIRIT

There cannot be two captains at the helm of our lives. Either we will be in control or Christ will. We must give our life to God, die to ourselves, crucify the flesh, and let Christ be our Captain. We have to stop walking in the flesh! If we insist on running our own life, if we choose to follow our own ambitions and desires, if we choose to do our own will, we will be disqualified from walking in the Spirit. Only the guidance of the Holy Spirit will lead us to safety in the will of God.

Today, I challenge you to let yourself be guided by the Holy Spirit—to acknowledge His impressions and intuitions and to hear and obey His voice. God wants you to manifest His power on earth. He sent His Spirit to be your Guide, to make His will known and to reveal His plans. You just have to surrender and yield to Him. Empty yourself by giving up your selfish will, your self-centered ambitions, and your human reasoning, and let God live in you. The difference will be noticed by anyone who comes in contact with you.

If today you say, "Holy Spirit, I want You to help me with my prayers, my marriage, my business and finances, and everything else," then He will guide you, and His influence in you will become stronger. He will place a desire in your heart to seek Him, to renounce your flesh, and to yield to Him. This is how you will become spiritually empowered and have a clear sense of direction in your life.

> ## The Christian walk demands that you crucify your flesh and surrender yourself to God.

ACTIVATION

"For as many as are led by the Spirit of God, these are sons of God" (Romans 8:14). When the Scripture says *"sons of God,"* it refers to mature believers who understand the importance of being led by the Spirit. Many people have never heard the voice of God, and this says something about the level of their spiritual growth. Immature believers do not know the voice of the Holy Spirit; they have never learned how to hear it, and that is why they cannot be led by Him. In order to become mature children of God, we have to know how to be constantly guided by Him.

We need to leave our childish ways behind and seek God more than ever before, so we can hear His voice clearly in the midst of these evil, demonic, and dangerous times. It is essential for the survival of the church that the children of God be led by His Spirit, because that is how we will conquer new territories for the kingdom and move from glory to glory.

Pray this prayer out loud:

Heavenly Father, Your Word says Your sheep hear Your call and follow You. You are my Shepherd, and You are my Father. As Your child, I know Your voice. In the name of Jesus Christ,

I repent for disobeying You, and I ask You to forgive me for all the times I have not heard or obeyed the intuitions, the impressions, or the inner testimonies of Your Spirit. Today, I deny myself, surrendering my insecurities, my fears, and my problems; I surrender the natural to receive the supernatural by the law of exchange. No longer do I live, but Christ lives in me. Holy Spirit, I crucify my flesh and invite You to fill, control, influence, and saturate my inner being with Your presence. I surrender my mind, my emotions, and my will so that You will become more real to me than everything else in my life. I die to the old man, to the old nature, and to ungodly desires. I stop walking in the flesh in order to walk in the Spirit. I am now ready to receive Your guidance.

Right now, I am filled with the Holy Spirit in all areas that have been under the control of my flesh. Father, I thank You and ask Your Holy Spirit to lead me supernaturally in my family, my work, and my ministry. I want You to guide me in all areas of my life! I receive the fullness and influence of the Holy Spirit. I decrease so that You may increase in me. I crucify myself so that You may live in and through me. I thank You, Father, in the name of Jesus. Amen!

8

THE RIVER, THE WAVES, AND THE FLOW OF THE SPIRIT

As the body of Christ, the church is entering one of the most beautiful times of its history—the greatest outpouring of the Holy Spirit that the earth has ever seen, in preparation for Christ's return. It is important for us to recognize the trends and patterns that will lead us to grow and to flow correctly with this great spiritual revival. The Holy Spirit is the expression of God on the earth, and without Him we cannot know what operations the Lord is initiating or where He is leading us. If we want to experience the movements of God, we need to hear what the Spirit is saying in the now. (See, for example, Revelation 2:7.) We must be aware of how the Holy Spirit flows today, both in the church and throughout the rest of the earth.

KEYS FOR UNDERSTANDING THE MOVEMENTS OF THE HOLY SPIRIT

The recorded vision of the prophet Ezekiel includes this passage:

Again he measured one thousand and brought me through the waters; the water came up to my knees. Again he measured one thousand and brought me through; the water came up to my waist. Again he measured one thousand, and it was a river that I could not cross; for the water was too deep, water in which one must swim.

(Ezekiel 47:4–5)

The Holy Spirit is like the water in a river that eventually covers us as we enter deeper and deeper into it, until the only way across is to swim. That is how our relationship with Him should be; we must be completely submerged in His power, presence, and manifestation, until we can swim in the river of His presence and follow each new wave and movement that He brings to the earth. The following are keys for understanding the river, the waves, and the flow of the Holy Spirit.

Every revival is out of our control because it comes from the Spirit.

1. THE RIVER OF THE SPIRIT COMES FROM THE THRONE OF GOD

"And he showed me a pure river of water of life, clear as crystal, proceeding from the throne of God and of the Lamb" (Revelation 22:1). The river of the Spirit carries activity from the throne of God to the earth and flows back to it. Those who are spiritually near the throne of God and know what the Spirit is saying today can understand the activity of the river. If

we do not know the throne or the river that flows from it, the movements of the Holy Spirit will not make sense to us. The work of the Spirit of God will go over our heads because it does not fit in with our personal agendas.

Pastors and other leaders, if you believe it is hard for people to receive the river of the Holy Spirit through the assignment God has given to you, you need to radically change your way of thinking. Revival *is* coming to various cities of the United States, Europe, Africa, Latin America, and the rest of the world. There are prophetic streams, rivers of holiness, deliverance, prosperity, healings, miracles, and creative miracles flowing from the throne of God, and the Spirit is waiting for you to open the door and allow His river to flow through your territory. Whenever I go to another church to minister, I make sure that the pastors have received the spirit of revival, because if they have not, it will be impossible for the movement of the Spirit to continue there. Remember that every pastor is the door of their church; they are the person who either allows or stops that which comes from God. For this reason, revival must begin in the life of the pastor; otherwise, they will close the door on the flow of the Holy Spirit.

You cannot carry a revival you do not participate in. That is why you need to jump into the river of the Spirit!

Sometimes people try to clone revivals that have occurred in other times or places, but they lack the true movement of the Spirit. It is possible to copy the forms of God, the way things have been done before, but the movement of the Spirit of God can never be cloned because the Holy Spirit has something different for each time, country, region, and

196 DIVINE ENCOUNTER WITH THE HOLY SPIRIT

believer. We need to discern the movements that the Lord has for our life and area and then become part of them in order to carry them in our spirit to share with others. The movements of the Spirit can only be felt or discerned when we participate in them.

For the Spirit's river to manifest, the *logos* and the *rhema* must work together. As we saw previously, the *logos* is the written Word, inspired by the Holy Spirit, that establishes the doctrine of our faith; but what is written remains inert until it is revealed to us through a *rhema* word. A *rhema* is a spoken word of God for today, for a specific situation; it is the *logos* revealed in the now. The *logos* is the basis upon which the river of the Holy Spirit is established, and the *rhema* is what carries the movements of the Spirit. Every movement of the Spirit begins with a *rhema* based on the *logos*.

Do you want to participate in the next revival on earth? Enter the river of the Spirit that is flowing in the now. There is no excuse for us not to allow the Spirit to move in our lives and ministries.

The *logos* is the basis upon which the river of the Spirit flows, but the *rhema* carries the movements of the Spirit of God.

2. THE HOLY SPIRIT'S NATURE IS ONE OF CONSTANT MOVEMENT

Since the beginning of creation, the Spirit has constantly been moving. (See, for example, Genesis 1:2.) God's Spirit never stands still because His nature is infinite, as is His ability to move. In the early church of the first century, the Holy Spirit remained in continual movement and expansion. To this day, the Spirit moves without ceasing, according to His eternal nature. He is always doing something and continuing to expand.

God can do something fresh every day, and in every moment, for the rest of eternity. There is always something new about God that He wants to do in us and through us, generation after generation. An individual who goes after God and after the next movement of the Spirit will never get bored, become complacent, or grow familiar with the anointing, because they will never want to miss what God will do next.

The spirit realm never remains static, because the Holy Spirit is always moving.

3. THE HOLY SPIRIT MOVES INSIDE OF US

When we receive the Holy Spirit, we are meant to flow in the eternal rivers that come from within us. Remember that on the "last and great day" of the Jews' Feast of Tabernacles, Jesus said, *"He who believes in Me, as the Scripture has said, out of his heart will flow rivers of living water.' But this He spoke concerning the Spirit, whom those believing in Him would receive"* (John 7:38–39). Our heart is the place where the Spirit of God dwells in us; He flows from deep within, in our innermost spirit. Often, we expect a revival to come from outside of us, for a special man or woman of God to impact us; but the Holy Spirit is already inside of us, waiting for us to step into His river. Remember that you and I flow with the same Spirit that Jesus Christ, Peter, Paul, and all of the first apostles did. And these are the days when the streams of the Spirit will flow from within us to minister to the world.

In the above passage, the work of the Spirit of God is compared to "*rivers*" because, again, the movement flows constantly, carrying His life. It is not a swamp of stagnant, dark, or putrid water, where nothing can live. Many religious people have turned their spiritual life into a swamp, so that there is no life inside them. Today, you must decide between yielding to the rivers of the Holy Spirit, which are full of healings, deliverances, transformation, prosperity, blessings, and miracles, or the swamp of religiosity and spiritual lukewarmness. I encourage you to choose the rivers of the Spirit!

4. THE HOLY SPIRIT MOVES IN THE DIMENSION OF SOUND

"*When the Day of Pentecost had fully come, they were all with one accord in one place. And suddenly there came a sound from heaven, as of a rushing mighty wind*" (Acts 2:1–2). Everything from God comes through the dimension of sound. His voice creates, bringing things into existence (see, for example, Genesis 1:3) and also upholding them (see Hebrews 1:3). Nothing in creation was formed until He spoke it into being.

Thus, the revelation of new life is in sound. To use an example from the physical world, when a woman wants to know the state of the life she carries in her womb, the first thing the doctor does is identify the presence of a heartbeat through an ultrasound scan. The Bible teaches us that our faith is prompted by the sounds of the Spirit, because it is written that "*faith comes by hearing, and hearing by the word of God*" (Romans 10:17). This principle is also seen during church services as God initially moves in the sounds and songs of worship, the Spirit speaking through human vessels.

In this season, God is lifting up people whose voices can release the river of the Spirit in various ways, and we must not confuse their voices with other voices that seem to come from the Spirit but are nothing more than echoes. The voice of God in a person will be genuine only when that person is approved and anointed by Him. When a voice is original, no one else can produce exactly what that voice produces. If the voice has the supernatural substance of the Spirit of God, then tangible and visible signs will follow.

We must keep in mind that God has no requirement regarding the background of the person He uses in this way; they might come from a village or a city, a poor country or a rich country; they might be an intellectual or they might be uneducated. Regardless, if the person is approved and anointed by God, nothing can stop the river of the Spirit from flowing through them. The devil cannot go against the voice that carries the present movement of the Spirit of God.

Thus, this is no time for us to turn to human formulas but rather to jump into the river of the Spirit and participate in the power and revival of God. Our voices, inspired by the Holy Spirit, will bring that revival!

What makes a movement of the Spirit authentic is the sound that comes from the mouth of God.

5. THE HOLY SPIRIT MOVES IN STREAMS AND WAVES

During the second half of the twentieth century, there were various moves of the Spirit in the church. In the sixties there was an evangelistic stream with healings and outstanding miracles. In the seventies and eighties there was a stream of the Spirit that brought a restoration of the prophetic gifts. In the nineties there was a stream of deliverance and prosperity; on top of this, there was a restoration of the apostolic ministry, which brought order and government to the church; and finally there was a strong stream of joy in the Spirit. Then, in the first decade of the twenty-first century, the world saw a stream of the glory of God and the manifestation of supernatural signs. The sad thing is that many leaders became used to one or two of these streams and just stayed there, without jumping into subsequent waves of the Spirit, including God's movements today. When the Holy Spirit is flowing, what sustains this stream is the grace of God. If His grace lifts or stops, we can safely say that the river of the Spirit has stopped. The moment that the grace of God leaves us or our ministry, the river of anointing and miracles stops flowing, and what remains is a ritual—an appearance of God without any power.

The Lord has allowed me to see incredible things as I have ministered, and the key to this has been my desire to flow in the new streams of His Spirit. That is why I place so much importance on discerning His streams and recognizing the direction that the next wave will take. Let me illustrate this with something that happened at the most recent Apostolic and Prophetic Conference (CAP) hosted by King Jesus Ministry. I heard the Holy Spirit say He would manifest His presence over His people in three different waves. The first wave would be of power, the second of holiness, and the third of love. And this is what I declared in front of over eighteen thousand people from more than a hundred nations.

When the wave of power came, we saw miracles, deliverances, manifestations of angels, and healings; people left their wheelchairs and rose up whole, and organs were created in people who needed them. When that wave finished, I released the wave of holiness, which brought conviction of sin to many people; I imparted the fear of God among them, and they repented for having offended Him. Many of them had grieved and quenched the Holy Spirit, but their repentance brought a transformation in their hearts, and they had supernatural encounters with the presence of God. Finally, I proclaimed the third wave, and the love of the Father came upon the arena where we were gathered. He healed the brokenhearted, the offended, and the hurt. His love poured out so strongly in that moment that miracles took place in people's marriages and in their relationships with the heavenly Father. All who were there—both men and women, young and old—received a personal touch from God.

How did I know it was God's will for the Holy Spirit to come in waves over the people with three different purposes? I came to know it as I prayed for the conference beforehand, when the Spirit of God spoke to me and showed me the direction He would take that night. I knew it because I know His nature and the way He operates; above all, I recognize His voice when He speaks to me. I have received this type of revelation over the many years of my ministerial life. The same thing happens when I prepare for the annual Supernatural Fivefold Ministry School (SFMS) that we host for leaders who make up the New Wine Apostolic Network. It also happens in the Supernatural Encounters that we hold not only in various cities in the United States, but also in many other countries. The Holy Spirit touches the hearts of thousands. As a result, we see incredible miracles and transformed lives. Be open to the streams and waves that God wants to reveal and minister!

> The Spirit of God moves in streams and waves whenever He is going to say, reveal, or do something new.

6. THE FLOW OF THE SPIRIT'S RIVER IS OMNIPRESENT, ETERNAL, AND INEXHAUSTIBLE

The Holy Spirit is not limited to the inside of our church walls; He can move anywhere. The Spirit of God is at our homes and jobs; He is with us in parking lots, malls, and everywhere else we go.

The stream of the Spirit is also eternal and inexhaustible, and once we receive it we feel that it flows and flows without limits; I often have this experience. Even after we have finished a service where we have let the river of the Spirit flow, it continues to move in me and speak to me. The same thing happens for many of those present. I usually feel a fire in my whole being that goes home with me. That is why, although I enjoy spending time with my brothers in Christ, sometimes I prefer not to go out with a large group to eat after a service; if I do, I go with just a few people so as to continue in that stream of the Spirit.

Something extraordinary along these lines happened to me while ministering in Norway. One night, I taught about encountering the Holy Spirit, and then I ministered a wave of God's glory. It fell on all the people, and it was glorious. After the service ended, I went to a room with the team that accompanied me. As soon as we entered, everyone began to weep in the presence of God. The movement of the Spirit continued, and we had a wonderful encounter with the Holy Spirit. The team cried, wept, and prostrated themselves before God. To this day, they tell me that they had never experienced anything like this before, and the fruit of that encounter has been seen in the transformation they experienced in their lives.

The Holy Spirit is not limited by time, space, or matter; He transcends them.

OBSTACLES THAT PREVENT THE SPIRIT FROM MOVING AND HIS RIVER FROM FLOWING

We must be aware of the obstacles that will daily come into our lives and threaten to stop the flow of the Holy Spirit inside us and keep us from touching the people who need His blessing. It's very important for us to identify these obstacles and remove them as they develop. Here are some of the most significant obstacles.

A RIGID, STRUCTURED, ORGANIZATIONAL MENTALITY

As we have seen, when a church operates according to human plans and laws, rather than according to the Spirit's leading, it becomes overly structured and rigid. That is why most churches and ministries today do not accommodate the new and the spontaneous that flows from the Spirit.

In any organization, it is good to have a certain structure in place that will help to facilitate the natural and administrative duties that must be carried out; but it is a mistake to think that the Spirit has to submit to this rigidity. We can never attribute disorder or chaos to the Holy Spirit; in fact, where there is disorder, He orders all things. It is best to have a flexible structure that balances the running of the natural organization with the supernatural movement of the Holy Spirit. We must learn to flow with Him so that He can release what God has planned for the natural structure.

That is why one of my constant prayers is, "Holy Spirit, I make room for You to move freely." Hence, in the church services at King Jesus Ministry, we always have time for the Word, but we also make room for the Holy Spirit to bring us His life, so we will not become a dead ministry. There have been times when people have interrupted one of our services because they were touched by the Holy Spirit. For example, I was preaching one day when suddenly I heard shouts coming from one section of the congregation. A woman came to the altar wanting to give her testimony. She said that she had been in a wheelchair for fifteen years because of a bone disease that prevented her from walking, but as I preached, she had been touched by the power of the Holy Spirit. Suddenly she felt strength in her legs, and she got up and was able to walk! I was not angry at this interruption; on the contrary, I stopped everything to hear the testimony and praised God for this instantaneous miracle. If I had tried to keep a certain structure to the service and rigidly followed it, I would not have given room for the Spirit of God to move or for a testimony to be given to edify the other believers. If we accommodate the spirit of religion, even when we do not mean to, we will lose the flow of God.

When the Holy Spirit comes, our traditions, routine actions, and religion disappear. We need to discern what He is doing in the now because, as Jesus told Martha, *"One thing is needed…"* (Luke 10:42), and that is to sit at the feet of Jesus and listen to what He wants us to discern and do today. We need to make room for the Holy Spirit to move among us, and we must keep an open mind about any new thing He wants to do or any new direction He wants to go in. I encourage you to release the Spirit's power in your life, in your congregation, and everywhere else He wants to do something supernatural.

OFFENSE OVER THE VESSEL THAT CARRIES THE ANOINTING

When we allow the stream of the Holy Spirit to flow, we will inevitably offend someone. However, the apostle Paul was very clear about the need to follow God rather than to please people. He told the Galatians, *"For do I now persuade men, or God? Or do I seek to please men? For if I still pleased men, I would not be a bondservant of Christ"* (Galatians 1:10).

Let us be careful that we do not take offense at the work of the Spirit or the vessels through whom He flows. As we saw in Luke 4, the problem of the religious leaders of the synagogue was that they were offended by Jesus; they could never receive from Him because the anointing that comes from a vessel that offends us will always be blocked from flowing to us. Those religious leaders refused to change their interpretations, traditions, and rules. According to them, if God wanted to do something, He would have to conform to their rules, respect their interpretations, and use only those people who met their approval. Let us not imitate them but rather be open to both God's movements and His chosen vessels.

THE ATTITUDE THAT WE ALREADY KNOW EVERYTHING WE NEED TO KNOW

We have seen that most religious leaders teach about God, but they do not demonstrate His power. When preachers lack the life of the Spirit, their words have no weight. Even after hearing them preach, you cannot say you have learned anything; you do not feel that you were given a message of value, one that can change your life, transform your reality, or help you see God's power in the midst of your insurmountable problems.

These religious leaders have too plain an image of the Lord, as though He were one-dimensional. They do not understand His *"width and length and depth and height"* (Ephesians 3:18); they don't receive revelation of anything new of the manifold wisdom and grace of the Spirit. (See Ephesians 3:10; 1 Peter 4:10.)

You may still wonder why the religious people of Jesus' time remained in a condition of stagnation. In my opinion, it is because they felt they already knew everything, that they had already spiritually "arrived." They believed that no one could teach them anything new or better about God. From being guardians of the Word, they became guardians of their own wisdom and rules. Nothing is more dangerous than believing we have reached a certain level of spirituality where we no longer need to seek revelation or anointing, or believing we can forget the flow of the Spirit.

As I described earlier, until the last century, the ministry gifts of apostles and prophets, who are biblically responsible for bringing the revelation of the supernatural and the Word of God in the present day, had been excluded from the leadership and activity of the church. The church only had teachers, evangelists, and pastors who taught the letter of the Word without manifestations of power. Therefore, the river of the Spirit ceased to flow in most of our congregations. Today, God has restored the activity of these ministries to the body of Christ, but many church leaders and denominations are still living according to the old ways of doing things. They too need to jump into the river of the Spirit!

HOW THE HOLY SPIRIT MOVES IN AND THROUGH US

At this point, I want to teach you how to allow the Spirit to move in and through you so that you can walk in His works, here and now. How does the Holy Spirit move in us?

BY OUR FAITH, WHICH WE EXERCISE

"For we walk by faith, not by sight" (2 Corinthians 5:7). Generally, we see that the Spirit of God moves in services where the people worship Him and where the pastor preaches and ministers to people with spiritual anointing, oil, and the laying on of hands under God's manifest presence. However, many times I have had to operate solely on raw faith, without the manifest presence of the Lord. In these times, I don't *feel*, perceive, or hear anything from God. However, I act in faith anyway because I know that God wants to heal and deliver His people, and the Holy Spirit honors that.

Faith does not reject reality but rather moves in the realm of the truth about Jesus and His victory through the cross, which we access through our imagination. Our imagination can see what our reason cannot validate. Sometimes I have seen the most powerful miracles when I have walked by faith while ministering in the midst of a heavenly atmosphere that was present even though unperceived.

Again, our imagination is not subject to the limits of reason, and that is why the Holy Spirit can use it to show us our true spiritual reality, or the highest truth. For example, if someone is missing an organ, their reason tells them they will never have it again because it is impossible in the natural for us to simply regrow an organ. However, if your imagination can see a new organ, and you believe that God can regrow it, the Lord can create it. This is what your faith is anchored to when God releases a creative miracle. In order for the Holy Spirit to move according to our faith, we must be confident that all things are possible for Him. (See, for example, Mark 9:23.)

Faith is the entry point to move in the supernatural. Everything that God does through you begins in faith.

BY THE ANOINTING, WHICH WE DEVELOP

The anointing is the power of God operating through us to heal, deliver, save, and prosper. God anoints us for the purpose of making known the gospel of Jesus Christ and establishing His kingdom on the earth. That is why it's so important for us to develop the anointing we have received. What have you done with the power you have received from God? If the anointing in you is not used, it will diminish.

Remember, the Holy Spirit is inside of you, but He will not operate until you prompt Him. Paul told Timothy, *"Therefore I remind you to stir up the gift of God which is in you through the laying on of my hands"* (2 Timothy 1:6). You must stir up the anointing inside you and work to make it continuously stronger. Consider this example from the physical world. When two liquids are mixed, the heavier one will sink to the bottom; the mixture needs to be stirred in order for that heavier liquid to rise up. A similar thing happens with the anointing. It is there, but we must stir it up to allow it to manifest. There is a dimension inside of you that has not yet been stirred up; it is still dormant. If you are walking in a spiritual drought and nothing is working for you, stir up the anointing of the Holy Spirit!

A powerful key to cultivating your anointing is a life of prayer and fasting. Jesus walked in the anointing because He always took time out to separate Himself from others to fast and to worship the Father. If you do the same, you will see the anointing of the Spirit of God move in and through your life to heal, deliver, prophesy, and minister to those who need a word from the Lord.

Another important key regarding the anointing is that the Holy Spirit flows with our God-given personality to empower us to manifest His life. Our personality connects with Him, and He produces a unique and personal way of expressing Himself through us. If our character is very hard, He softens it; or if it is very soft, He affirms it—but He does not fundamentally change it. He just wants to mold us so His faith and anointing can flow through us.

Now that you understand how the anointing of the Spirit works, begin to use the anointing that is in you. Stir it up, bring it to the surface, and when you feel it activated in you, go and lay hands on people who desire that. Preach the Word and manifest the power of God by healing the sick and casting out demons!

FLOWING WITH THE SPIRIT

A question many Christians ask about the movement of the Holy Spirit is, "How can we understand what the Spirit wants, and how can we flow in what He desires to do today?" To flow with the river of the Spirit, we must understand His direction and be ready to change.

Nothing happens randomly in the spiritual world. The Holy Spirit moves in a specific direction, with a previously defined purpose.

UNDERSTAND HIS DIRECTION

The Holy Spirit never moves randomly or by chance but always follows the specific direction given by the Father, just as He did with Jesus. At any moment, He may move in a wave of creative miracles, in the glory of God, in healings, in a prophetic river to affirm people's callings or confirm decisions, or in releasing the supernatural on a church that is advancing in revelation. He always has a direction in which He wants to go, with a previously defined purpose. Remember that in the days of Moses, God's glory always moved in a direction that was marked by a pillar of fire by night and a massive cloud by day. (See, for example, Exodus 13:21.) As we have seen, at that time God moved in the physical dimension because the people were spiritually dead. They did not yet know the Lord or His ways, and thus He took visible forms to reveal

Himself. Today, He does not need to guide us by a pillar of fire or cloud because the Holy Spirit dwells within us. But in the river of the Spirit there is always a direction that we must recognize in order to flow with the new things of the Spirit for each occasion.

When I preach, it frequently happens that I can feel in what section of the congregation there is the strongest spiritual activity, as well as where the people are placing the greatest demand on God by their faith and seeking. The Holy Spirit always responds to the needs of those who are hungry and thirsty for Him. When I tell the people in which direction the Holy Spirit is moving, they can align themselves with Him and direct their hunger to what is available from heaven at that time.

Every church leader must know how to watch, see, and discern the direction in which the Holy Spirit is moving. That is why a prophetic worship leader is needed, as Chenaniah was in David's tabernacle (see 1 Chronicles 15:22); we need someone who can lead the worship and discern the direction of the Spirit of God, recognizing where He is heading.

As we seek to follow God's Spirit, let us keep in mind that the movement of the Holy Spirit makes no distinction with regard to people's gender, age, or race. He works in the lives of blacks, whites, Latinos, Asians, Native Americans, and every other race, whether they are male or female, young or old. He manifests freely among those in every continent, tongue, and culture on earth who discern His presence.

> **We must discern the direction the Holy Spirit is moving in our lives, our churches, and the entire world.**

BE READY TO CHANGE

In our walk with Christ, we need an environment that will lead us to permanent change so that we may live in continuous growth from season to season. We must move from one level of revelation to another, from one level of death to the "old man" to a greater level, from one level of anointing to another.

Change is often painful, but when we reject it there comes a time when the residue of our old anointing starts to stink. This is what happens when people decide to remain the same, not seeking something new from God and not pouring themselves into the lives of others. That is why the Scriptures say, *"Cursed is he who does the work of the LORD deceitfully.... Moab has been at ease from his youth; he has settled on his dregs, and has not been emptied from vessel to vessel.... Therefore his taste remained in him, and his scent has not changed"* (Jeremiah 48:10–11).

Most people either do not want to change or don't recognize their need for it. However, the Spirit of God comes to give life to a dead environment. If He is given room to flow in our churches, our services will always be marked by the life of the Spirit. The praise, worship, preaching, and ministration will be full of His life. Thus, for a Christian, change is a condition for living in the permanent "now" of God. But what specifically do we need to change? We can start with the following.

When the Holy Spirit manifests, there is life, and what's dead is raised again.

WE MUST CHANGE OUR MENTALITY

"For 'who has known the mind of the LORD that he may instruct Him?' But we have the mind of Christ" (1 Corinthians 2:16). Everyone who has received the mind of Christ has undergone transformation; they have changed or renewed their thoughts to align with His. (See Romans

12:2.) To flow in the Spirit, therefore, we need to change the way we think about God and how He works.

WE MUST CHANGE OUR WAY OF PRAYING

When the Holy Spirit dwells within us, He reveals to us that we are children of God. When we receive that revelation, our prayer life changes; we no longer petition from the standpoint of a beggar, but we make declarations as children of God who know how to receive our inheritance and activate the power of the Spirit with our voices. In addition, we learn to enter God's presence with gratitude, worshipping in spirit and truth (see John 4:23–24) and becoming more intimate with our heavenly Father. In the process, the character of Christ grows in us.

WE MUST CHANGE OUR PRAISE AND WORSHIP

When the presence of the Holy Spirit is activated inside us, the sounds that are playing in heaven immediately begin to flow there. The praise of heaven is always about what God wants to release on earth, and our spirit will identify with it. That is why we cannot continue to praise the Lord with the songs of the last century; we need to change and renew our praise, to declare the mighty works that God is doing today. This does not mean that old songs or praises are bad but that they were good for a particular season and for a movement of the Spirit that has already passed.

Accordingly, we must bring new life to our praise for the Lord as the Holy Spirit leads us. Today is a new day, and so will tomorrow be. In order for something new to come, we have to bring new songs from the throne of God—what is playing in heaven today—exalting the name of Jesus and His finished work on the cross, His majesty, and His power.

Likewise, we need to change our worship. If we say that we have intimacy with God, but our songs speak more of us than of Him; if they talk more about our humanity, emotions, needs, or conditions than of our love and devotion to God, we urgently need to renew and redirect our worship.

> When you exchange the old songs for new songs from the throne of God, you have a new connection to the flow and atmosphere of heaven.

WE MUST CHANGE THE WAY WE LISTEN

We must also change the way we listen when we worship and pray by listening for sounds and revelation from heaven. Moreover, when someone truly desires change, they will listen closely to, and receive, the Word proclaimed by the pastor or teacher; they will treasure it and make it theirs right away, applying it to their lives. God's Word should not go in one ear and out the other. It must be planted in our hearts and manifest as fruit in our lives.

WE MUST CHANGE OUR ENVIRONMENT

To begin, I must make clear that an environment is not the same as an atmosphere. Environment is what's already present, while spiritual atmosphere is created. In this sense, heaven is an environment, but the throne of God is an atmosphere, and it can be brought to the earth and manifested. A spiritual atmosphere is built by praise, worship, prayer, speaking in tongues, declarations of miracles and healings, and more. In heaven, the *"four living creatures"* come together and praise the Lord, saying, *"Holy, holy, holy, Lord God Almighty, who was and is and is to come!"* (Revelation 4:8). Wherever there is an atmosphere of worship, the Lord constantly reveals something new, and the environment carries His life.

By definition, an environment requires that we interact with it. If the environment of your revival "stream" has not changed for years, a new movement of the Spirit of God cannot flow through you, because you think, speak, and act according to that old environment. I know of many churches that have tried to have the movement of the Spirit that flows in our ministry, but they have had no success. They have made the mistake of attempting to keep their old environment, using the same songs, preaching, and rigid processes of the past, which are obsolete and out of touch with what God is saying today. Jesus said that one does not put new wine in old wineskins. (See, for example, Mark 2:22.) In other words, the Holy Spirit will not move in the now if you still live in the environment of the past.

Every time God calls someone, He takes them out of their environment.

Most leaders cannot exercise their anointing when they find themselves trying to minister in a dead spiritual environment. They feel bound, the power of God does not activate in them, and they do not know what to do. The solution is for them to learn to invite the atmosphere of the Spirit. They must first penetrate the darkness with praise to the Lord, entering spiritual warfare to remove the principalities and powers of spiritual death, religiosity, oppression, and darkness. From there, they need to build the throne of God, or His presence, on earth, by worshipping in spirit and truth according to the prophetic direction of the Spirit. When the movement of the Holy Spirit comes, the first thing the Spirit does is to testify about Jesus; thus, they must become aligned with this testimony, so that the Spirit's anointing can flow from within them, manifesting a new atmosphere of life and miracles.

For example, when I go somewhere to minister and the environment is dry and dead, I know I need to interact with that environment. I begin to work with the atmosphere through music, and I use people's Spirit-inspired voices to bring the new atmosphere of the life of the Spirit to that dead environment. My band of musicians and prophetic worshippers help me to generate an atmosphere of living, vibrant, and present worship that allows the Spirit to flow with new revelation from heaven. Thus, the atmosphere changes and becomes a "new wineskin," into which the new wine of the Spirit can be poured.

Let us create a new atmosphere in the renewed environments of our churches and ministries where we allow freedom for the Spirit of God to move with power!

ACTIVATION

Say this prayer out loud:

Heavenly Father, I thank You for the gift that is Your Holy Spirit. I repent for any way in which I have prevented or stopped the Spirit's flow in my life and ministry. I repent for having a structured and rigid mentality, and I ask that the river of Your Spirit be constantly moving in me. Wash me and baptize me in Your waters, because I do not want to be a stagnant spiritual swamp. I renounce every religious spirit in me. I cast it out, and I open my mind and my spirit to be filled with You. I ask that You give me the wisdom to know the Spirit's nature and the grace to follow His movements. Right now, I receive a fresh anointing from You.

Lord, help me to discern when You are going to say or reveal something, and to be available and obey Your voice. Whisper to me the revealed word for today, so that I may jump into Your river. Today I choose to take steps of faith wherever I go—to pray for the sick and to cast out demons. I will empty myself into people, giving them everything You have given me. I will activate them, heal them, and deliver them for Your glory.

Help me to create an atmosphere where the Spirit moves with freedom, power, and glory. Teach me to move in the different streams and waves of power, deliverance, healing, riches, restoration, inner healing, and fire in order to change and transform lives. Move in my life, in my family, in my ministry, and in every other environment I am in. Father, give me Your grace to walk with You in the now, so others can see my relationship with You. From this moment on, I follow the river, the waves, and the flow of Your Spirit. In the name of Jesus, amen!

KEEP SEEKING DIVINE ENCOUNTERS

We live in an age of many deceitful powers, numerous crises, and much faithlessness. Today more than ever, we need to be filled with the Holy Spirit, power, and fire in order to demonstrate a living God who is willing to reveal Himself in divine encounters and show Himself faithful in the midst of the problems of His people.

HAVE CONTINUOUS FELLOWSHIP WITH THE SPIRIT

Paul prayed for the church in Corinth to have fellowship with the Holy Spirit, saying, *"The grace of the Lord Jesus Christ, and the love of God, and the communion of the Holy Spirit be with you all"* (2 Corinthians 13:14). Paul knew that in the midst of our intimate relationship with the Spirit, there is an exchange where we renounce ourselves and surrender everything to God and where God imparts Himself to us; when we have communion with the Holy Spirit, we become one with Him and assimilate all that He has. Today, I encourage you to have continuous fellowship with the Holy Spirit so that, through encounters with Him, you will be transformed by His power and love.

As I stated at the beginning of this book, some encounters with God are sovereign, while others can be initiated by us—and the Lord responds when we seek Him from our heart. If we set aside all religious conformity, customs, and traditions, and if we desire more of the Spirit of God, He will give us supernatural encounters.

HAVE CONTINUOUS HUNGER AND THIRST FOR GOD

We have seen that one of our great challenges is to remain both hungry for God and filled with Him at the same time. Hunger for the Lord never lets you be satisfied or fulfilled for long but instead leads you to insatiably desire more of Him. Hunger and thirst for His presence are signs of spiritual well-being, while demonstrating our humbleness before Him.

> **People who are hungry and thirsty leave their convenience and safety behind in order to seek more of God.**

Remember, God cannot take you beyond the level of your contentment. If you are content with what you have already seen of God, with what you know and have received from Him, you will not be able to see, know, or receive more. Without hunger for God, you cannot move from where you are to where you need to be; stagnation and irrelevance alone await you. No doubt, the Holy Spirit welcomes those who rush to seek Him and crave an encounter with Him. If you seek the Holy Spirit, He will fill you to the top of your contentment. If you remove all limitations, He will fill you more and more, and you will enter into the depths of His waters without ceasing.

A crisis always captures our attention, prompting us to seek God.

Often it is in the midst of impossible circumstances that great supernatural encounters occur. In the Bible we see impossible cases like Daniel being thrown into a pit of lions (see Daniel 6) or his friends being tossed into a fiery furnace, ready to be burned alive—all for refusing to worship a human king (see Daniel 3). But as they were going through these situations, Daniel and his friends had supernatural encounters with God in which they fellowshipped with Him and were brought through their dire situations. Likewise, many people today have had supernatural encounters with God when they were in the midst of an impossible situation, like a terminal illness; or when they were suffering a crisis, such as a divorce, a serious family problem, or a bankruptcy. In other words, the encounter came through a situation that only God could change. I know ministers who exhausted their resources and natural abilities trying to carry out a ministry, and only after going through a great crisis did they empty themselves and receive a face-to-face encounter with God and His Holy Spirit. Many of the spiritual children that God has given me came to King Jesus Ministry when they were suffering a crisis and were about to abandon everything. We received them, delivered them, and led them to have an encounter with the Holy Spirit. Today they are restored and impacting their territories with the supernatural power of God. What seemed impossible became possible, and it all happened after they had an encounter with the Holy Spirit.

THIS IS THE TIME FOR A DIVINE ENCOUNTER!

I declare that this is the time in which you will have a life-changing encounter with the Holy Spirit. I proclaim that just as Jesus, as a Man, was changed, empowered, and commissioned, so will you be. I encourage and challenge you to seek more of God than ever before, to search after Him beyond all that you have previously seen and known of Him. I dare you to long for more supernatural encounters with the Holy Spirit—to be empowered, activated, and commissioned for the purpose of doing all that Jesus did on earth, and more.

Do not wait any longer! This book is for you. This message is for you. Today is the time—God expects you to respond. Christ is coming soon. Prepare your heart through divine encounters with the Holy Spirit. I bless you in the mighty name of Jesus!

ABOUT THE AUTHOR

Apostle Guillermo Maldonado is the senior pastor and founder of King Jesus International Ministry (Ministerio Internacional El Rey Jesus), in Miami, Florida, a multicultural church considered to be one of the fastest growing in the United States. King Jesus Ministry, whose foundation is built upon the Word of God, prayer, and worship, currently has a membership of nearly seventeen thousand. The ministry also offers spiritual covering to a growing network of over three hundred churches that extends throughout the United States and globally in Latin America, Europe, Africa, Asia, and New Zealand, representing over six hundred thousand people. The building of kingdom leaders and the visible manifestations of God's supernatural power distinguish the ministry as the number of its members constantly multiplies.

Apostle Maldonado has authored over fifty books and manuals, many of which have been translated into other languages. His previous books with Whitaker House are *How to Walk in the Supernatural Power of God, The Glory of God, The Kingdom of Power, Supernatural Transformation,* and *Supernatural Deliverance,* all of which are available in both English and Spanish. In addition, he preaches the message of Jesus Christ and His redemptive power on his national and international television program, *The Supernatural Now (Lo Sobrenatural Ahora),* which airs on TBN, Daystar, the Church Channel, and fifty other networks, thus with a potential outreach and impact to more than two billion people across the world.

Apostle Maldonado has a doctorate in Christian counseling from Vision International University and a master's degree in practical theology from Oral Roberts University. He resides in Miami, Florida, with his wife and ministry partner, Ana, and their two sons, Bryan and Ronald.

Welcome to Our House!

We Have a Special Gift for You

It is our privilege and pleasure to share in your love of Christian books. We are committed to bringing you authors and books that feed, challenge, and enrich your faith.

To show our appreciation, we invite you to sign up to receive a specially selected **Reader Appreciation Gift**, with our compliments. Just go to the Web address at the bottom of this page.

God bless you as you seek a deeper walk with Him!

WE HAVE A GIFT FOR YOU. VISIT:

whpub.me/nonfictionthx

WHITAKER
HOUSE